the series on school reform

Patricia A. Wasley   Ann Lieberman   Joseph P. McDonald
University of Washington   Carnegie Foundation for the   New York University
                          Advancement of Teaching
                          SERIES EDITORS

(Continued)

the series on school reform, *continued*

MENTORS
in the
MAKING

Developing New Leaders
for New Teachers

Edited by
BETTY ACHINSTEIN
AND STEVEN Z. ATHANASES

Foreword by Ellen Moir

Teachers College, Columbia University
New York and London

Published by Teachers College Press, 1234 Amsterdam Avenue,
New York, NY 10027

Library of Congress Cataloging-in-Publication Data

Achinstein, Betty.
    Mentors in the making : developing new leaders for new teachers /
edited by Betty Achinstein and Steven Z. Athanases ; foreword by
Ellen Moir
        p.   cm.—(The series on school reform)
    Includes bibliographical references and index.
    ISBN-13: 978-0-8077-4636-3 (cloth : alk. paper)
    ISBN-10: 0-8077-4636-3 (cloth : alk. paper)
    ISBN-13: 978-0-8077-4635-6 (paper : alk. paper)
    ISBN-10: 0-8077-4635-5 (paper : alk.paper)
        1. Mentoring in education. 2. Teachers—training of. I. Athanases,
Steven Z. II. Title. III. The series on school reform (New York, N.Y.)
    LB1731.4 .M475 2006
    370.71/5—dc22   2005052983

ISBN-13:   ISBN-10:
978-0-8077-4635-6 (paper)   0-8077-4635-5 (paper)
978-0-8077-4636-3 (cloth)   0-8077-4636-3 (cloth)

Printed on acid-free paper
Manufactured in the United States of America

13 12 11 10 09 08 07 06   8 7 6 5 4 3 2

This book is dedicated to two of our greatest mentors:
Asher Achinstein (1900–1998), Betty's grandfather,
and Alexander T. Athanases (1923–2004), Steven's dad.

Contents

Foreword

Mentors in the Making makes a vital contribution to our profession. It explores the complex knowledge base of mentors working with novices, highlighting both promises and challenges in enacting a transformative vision of induction. It brings together voices of induction leaders, mentors, researchers, and professional developers all deeply concerned with launching a new generation of teachers. The image of such a launch captures much of the excitement and exuberance of new teachers along with the rather momentous endeavor involved in supporting them. Embarking on such a journey involves much preparation. This book provides critical insights to help navigate the often rough seas. But beyond helping navigate current waterways, this volume provides maps for envisioning and charting new directions. For the next generation of teachers, induction must envision a future that does not re-create the status quo where, all too often, new teachers and mentors encounter systems devoid of passion, caring, equity, and opportunities for human development. *Mentors in the Making* provides critical questions and a message of hope as we launch new teachers and mentors on their momentous and sometimes arduous expedition.

I am acutely aware of the passion, commitment, and expertise of outstanding educators who step forward to mentor new teachers. I have committed the last 20 years of my career to supporting quality induction because I believe it is the leverage point for change in our profession. At the same time, I wonder if our profession and organizations have learned how to utilize fully the potent resource of mentors or to provide systems necessary to help these talented veterans develop skills and professional leadership to capitalize on their potential.

We place the success of our next generation of teachers in the hands of these talented veteran teachers. It is an awesome responsibility and an enormous opportunity, but what exactly does this new role of beginning teacher mentor entail? How can we most effectively build on veteran teachers' knowledge and experience as they become teachers of teachers? How can we ensure that we support these veteran teachers in providing the highest-quality guidance and assistance possible? What sorts of systems welcome and acknowledge this role for what it is?

We are beginning to recognize that great teachers are not born but developed over time, and that there is a body of professional knowledge and standards of professional practice that underlie this development. It is also important for us to recognize that these same great teachers need time, careful professional development, and ongoing support to develop the new set of skills and understandings that will make them outstanding teachers of teachers.

Development of quality mentors has two important dimensions. First, it involves learning new, sometimes complex skills and understandings that are rarely intuitive. This means we need to begin asking questions like: What is the pedagogy of mentoring? What sort of curriculum best supports mentor development? And how best can we impart that curriculum? Second, these outstanding veterans need systems that accord them the status, time, and recognition to function in this demanding role while providing the ongoing support and development they need. We might ask: How do we capitalize upon this new role for teachers to influence our system? What structures need to be in place? What policies? And how do mentors (and the new teachers they induct) fit into our organization's greater vision for the teaching profession? Moreover, how can they transform educational systems to be more educational and equitable?

The implications of these new roles for veteran teachers are many, and the opportunity to influence our profession at both ends of the developmental continuum (novice and veteran) is exciting. *Mentors in the Making* brings to light the central concern of mentor development, the curriculum and pedagogy of mentoring, and the organizational contexts that foster powerful induction. In focusing on the mentors' roles and contexts, this book also advocates for a new kind of profession, one where mentors and teachers are critically reflective of their practices, focused on the needs of diverse learners, and oriented toward school reform. In this volume you will find new understandings about the knowledge, skills, and dispositions needed by mentors and induction leaders who will transform a new generation of educators.

—Ellen Moir

Acknowledgments

We first acknowledge Ellen Moir, executive director of the New Teacher Center at the University of California, Santa Cruz. It is her pioneering work, supported by the Center, that spawned the Leadership Network for Teacher Induction (LNTI), focus of much of the work reported in this book. LNTI was co-facilitated by Betty Achinstein, Janet Gless, and Barbara Davis, all from the Center, and funded by a generous grant from the William and Flora Hewlett Foundation. Projects whose voices and work are represented in this book include: MillsPLuS Consortium, New Haven Unified School District, Oakland Unified School District, San Jose Unified School District, San Mateo County Office of Education, San Mateo/Foster City School District, San Ramon Valley Unified School District, Santa Cruz New Teacher Project, Triple L Collaborative, Santa Clara County Office of Education, Santa Clara Unified School District, Palo Alto Unified School District/Mt. View–Los Altos High School District, and San Francisco Unified School District. We thank all of the mentors and induction leaders whose work and thinking contributed to this volume.

Several others supported these efforts. We acknowledge Ann Lieberman of the Carnegie Foundation for the Advancement of Teaching for her advocacy of this work and her support for the book. We thank Anna Richert of Mills College for her commitment to supporting inquiry in LNTI. Luciana Carvalho de Oliveira and Emilio Soltero contributed to data analysis in some chapters during their doctoral study at the University of California, Davis. We also acknowledge the helpful guidance of Susan Liddicoat at Teachers College Press and the critical feedback of anonymous reviewers who helped shape this work.

We could not have brought this book to fruition without the mentors who shaped our own early careers. We honor Doris Gelman, Betty's first teacher mentor, and Larry Cuban, who mentored Betty's research career. We also honor James Wicklund, Steven's high school department chair, and Beverly Whitaker Long, who ushered Steven into scholarship. Without their commitments to our early career development, we would not have developed images of the possible nor the capacity to bring them to print.

Finally, we recognize those who continue to sustain us throughout our lives, including our families and friends for their encouragement. Betty especially honors Chad and Adin Raphael for their love and compassion.

New Visions for Mentoring New Teachers

Betty Achinstein and Steven Z. Athanases

Betty's first year of teaching in a Chicago public school:

150 8th graders
40 different languages spoken
1 brand-new school, in a city undergoing school reform
4 competing gang territories from which students are bused to school
25 colleagues with competing views on teaching diverse youth
5 incomplete sets of social studies textbooks
10 burned-out (and never replaced) classroom lights in a gray
     Chicago winter
1 hope for a progressive school and the struggles to make it happen.

Steven's first year of teaching in Arlington Heights, Illinois:

150 high school students
120 freshmen nobody else seems to want to teach
4 sections of English composition (1 remedial level)
1 section of reading lab to team-teach with the "battle-axe" whom
     students and other teachers fear
10,000 pages of student writing to read in 9 months
30 9th graders who need to learn how to write a sentence

1 principal angry that a dictionary soared out the 2nd-floor window
10 all-day Saturday speech tournaments (1 bus caught in a blizzard
on the ride home)

These brief tallies of our early career challenges in public school teaching
were not, of course, unique. Nor were our first-year questions: How can I
meet the needs of all of my students? What and how should I teach? How
will I negotiate conflicts at school? Like many in the profession, we man-
aged to find veteran teachers to provide help. This support, however, was
seldom systematized, and it lacked a structure, a vision, and a knowledge
base about what we needed as new teachers, and when and why and how. A
quality mentoring and induction support system could have guided us in
moving from being students of teaching to quality teachers of students.

More recently, interest in new teacher support and induction programs
is growing as they are reported to yield increased teacher retention, improved
practice, and improved student achievement. Programs that pair a novice with
a mentor to provide professional development and guidance are proliferat-
ing internationally. However, much of what passes as mentoring is haphazard, falling short of ambitious educative aims. The dominant conception of
novices in "survival mode," focused on self-image and classroom control,
limits mentors' roles to emotional support or technical advice-giver. Yet new
teachers need more and different kinds of support in meeting ambitious educational reform goals for teachers of the 21st century. The nature of learning that is possible and needed during induction—and therefore the kinds of
knowledge, skills, and dispositions mentors need—requires rethinking. We
know little about what mentors need to know and be able to do to help
novices develop into quality professionals who have taken up reform-minded
teaching. Educators can no longer afford only a haphazard approach to the
induction of its newcomers, nor one with limited assumptions about new
teachers as learners. We lose too many teachers, often some of the best and
the brightest, too early in their careers. Students in classes of new teachers
too often get shortchanged. Clearly we need greater articulation of ambitious conceptions and models of induction and mentoring to address these
needs.

In response to growing interest and questions about mentoring and
teacher induction, we collaborated with practitioners and researchers to write
this book, which has three main goals:

1. To articulate a complex knowledge base of mentoring needed to
   foster quality teaching in the 21st century, one that focuses new
   teachers on reform-minded conceptions of teaching and learning,
   students, and the profession.

2. To explore how mentors' knowledge, skills, and dispositions can be developed effectively, examining a curriculum for mentor professional development.
3. To describe challenges and promising practices of mentoring in action.

Our title highlights key assumptions about the book. We refer to *mentors in the making* to emphasize that mentors are not born, but developed through conscious, deliberate, ongoing learning. We focus on *developing new leaders* to emphasize how mentors need new understandings, knowledge, and visions; thus the book features a new *kind* of leader. This part of the title foregrounds the importance of fostering new kinds of knowledge, complex understandings, skills, and dispositions that mentors must have at two levels, about students and about new teachers. The book spotlights challenges, using problems from the field as a way to inquire about the work of and conceptions about mentoring. It also examines practices, closely scrutinizing mentoring conversations, interactions, and field-tested tools to open up the "black box" of mentoring. Leadership for *new teachers* is the focus of this volume because guiding the novice during a key period of socialization—one that can inform a possible 40-year career—is a strategic leverage point to influence the profession.

This book offers educators, researchers, and policymakers descriptions and analyses of mentoring and induction from educators engaged in systematic inquiry, struggling for contexts that foster ambitious new teacher development, equitable learning opportunities for students, and systemic change. In this volume we use original empirical research, practitioner action inquiry, and field-tested practices. The volume highlights opportunities and challenges of mentoring within diverse educational contexts. These include urban and suburban schools, large and small districts, multidistrict consortia, school- and museum-based sites, and collaborations with universities and county offices of education.

A CALL FOR NEW TEACHER SUPPORT

In the first 10 years of the 21st century over two million new teachers are needed in the United States. Yet despite this staggering figure, attracting and hiring teachers is only the start. Addressing the revolving door of new teacher attrition is a more critical matter (Ingersoll, 2001a). Of those who enter the profession, approximately 30% leave within 3 years, and up to 50% leave within 5 years (Darling-Hammond, 1997; Ingersoll, 2002; Ingersoll & Smith, 2003b). Teachers in schools serving high-poverty communities have an even greater risk of leaving at the end of their first year (Smith & Ingersoll,

2004). Moreover, those identified as more academically able may be the most likely to leave (Murnane, Singer, Willet, Kemple, & Olsen, 1991; Schlechty & Vance, 1983). This early departure from the profession is due to factors such as job dissatisfaction and unsupportive schooling conditions (Ingersoll, 2001b; Johnson, 2004). Most teachers still experience the "sink-or-swim" career introduction, isolated in their classrooms, unsupported by colleagues, with little power over decisionmaking and few opportunities for learning. Some characterize the teaching profession as unique in "eating its young."

Beyond retention, developing the quality of new professionals is paramount. Recent research demonstrates the significant influence of teacher quality on student achievement (Hanushek, 1992; Rivkin, Hanushek, & Kain, 2005; Sanders & Rivers, 1996). The No Child Left Behind Act of 2001 requires that all teachers be "highly qualified," and concurrent accountability measures raise the bar of teacher expectations. Goals articulated by recent standards-based reforms call for complex teacher understandings and capacities. These include: a deep knowledge base (about learners and learning, curriculum and teaching, and social contexts of education); a repertoire of pedagogical skills; and use of knowledge and skills tailored to particular students, classes, schools, subject matter demands, and objectives (Darling-Hammond, Wise, & Klein, 1999). The bar for professional standards and knowledge has been raised. Standards like those of the Interstate New Teacher Assessment and Support Consortium (INTASC) outline knowledge, skills, and dispositions expected of new teachers that support ambitious and reform-minded teaching.

For new teachers with no teacher education or credential, challenges can intensify. In 2000–01, in California alone, more than 42,000 teachers, 14% of the workforce, did not hold preliminary or professional clear credentials (completed licensure) (Shields et al., 2001). Nearly half of new teachers in the state begin teaching before completing a preliminary teaching credential (California Department of Education, 2003). Moreover, unprepared teachers are unequally distributed to low-income, high-minority, and under-performing schools, among the most challenging settings for novices. In states like California, students in lowest-performing schools are about five times more likely to be taught by an underprepared teacher than students in high-performing schools (Shields et al., 2001).

The beginning teaching phase offers an opportunity to make or break the new professional and, ultimately, the profession. Conditions that shape the first years determine teacher effectiveness, attitudes and behaviors, and decisions to stay in the field (Bush, 1983). Fortunately, some educators in recent years began to see this phase as unique for fostering the professional norms that schools and students deserve, and that teachers need to believe in a viable future in the profession. Tasks of supporting and retaining the remarkable number of new teachers needed have generated widespread interest in induction and mentoring support. Such interest deepened as early evidence suggested that high-quality induction and mentoring programs yielded various benefits. These included improved teacher retention, job satisfaction, teaching quality, and ultimately student achievement (Fletcher, Strong, & Villar, 2004; Huling-Austin, 1990; Ingersoll & Smith, 2003a; National Commission on Teaching and America's Future, 1996; Odell & Ferraro, 1992; Pearson & Honig, 1992; Smith & Ingersoll, 2004; Strong & St. John, 2001; Wilson, Darling-Hammond, & Berry, 2001).[1]

Furthermore, calls for greater professionalism and accountability, whereby educators define professional standards and monitor their own, have generated a proliferation of induction programs. Interest in teacher induction has, in fact, grown worldwide. In the United States, while in the 1990–01 school year less than half of beginning teachers nationwide reported participating in an induction program, by the 1999–2000 school year, almost 80% of novices reported having a mentor or participating in an induction program (Smith & Ingersoll, 2004). As of 2003, 30 states had formal induction programs for 1 to 3 years; 16 required and financed formal induction for all new teachers (Quality counts, 2003). Some of these programs involve one-to-one mentor support aligned with professional standards, professional development seminars targeted for novices, networks of new teachers, and opportunities for observation and formative feedback on practice. Eight states required mentors and teachers to be matched by school, subject, and/or grade level; seven states required release time for mentors; and nine states required some form of compensation for mentors (Quality counts).

China, France, New Zealand, Switzerland, and Japan have well-funded induction support for 2 or more years addressing ambitious learning goals for new teachers (Britton, Paine, Pimm, & Raizen, 2003). In Israel, the Ministry of Education and Culture funds induction and mentor development (Orland, 2001). In Australia, educators and policymakers show increasing commitment to mentoring new teachers (Ballantyne, Hansford, & Packer, 1995). Clearly, many policymakers, reformers, and educators worldwide have turned their attention to teacher induction, given the need for new teachers, the support necessary to retain them, and an urgency to meet ambitious teaching goals articulated by reforms.

CONCEPTIONS OF INDUCTION AND MENTORING

Induction refers to three concepts: a unique phase as an individual transitions from being a student of teaching to becoming a teacher of students; a period of socialization into the norms of the profession; and formal programs and comprehensive systems of sustained support and professional development for teachers in their first few years in the profession (Feiman-Nemser, Schwille, Carver, & Yusko, 1999). *Mentoring* is a central strategy of many induction programs, which pairs the novice with an expert veteran teacher focused on supporting the novice's professional development. The term mentor comes from a character in Homer's *Odyssey* who educated and supported Telemachus while his father was away. The mentor was a wise guide invested in the personal development of the protégé. More recently, mentoring has been likened to an apprenticeship focused on occupational socialization linked to career development (Little, 1990). In new teacher education, the mentor may attend to the professional development of beginning teachers through ongoing observation, conversations and assessment of practice, goal-setting aligned with standards of quality teaching and subject matter knowledge, advocacy, and technical and emotional support. Mentors may model lessons, jointly plan curriculum, coach on subject matter content or pedagogy, collaboratively inquire, discuss individual learners and examine student work, read research, talk about navigating school issues, identify inequities in the classroom, and guide novices using a variety of approaches.

Limitations of Induction and Mentoring Conceptions and Practices

In practice, however, many induction and mentoring programs do not rest on robust ideas about teacher knowledge, students, or change (Feiman-Nemser et al., 1999). The most common form of new teacher support is still workshops typically focused on school policies and classroom management (Shields et al., 2001). Goals include easing newcomers' transition into existing school and district cultures and promoting teachers' retention. Induction programs and mentoring practice too often center on little more than teacher accountability through reductive tasks and checkoff lists as monitoring devices. Even programs with a mentoring component vary dramatically from comprehensive systems that support release time for mentors and novices to meet, aided by compensation and ongoing professional development, to more informal setups that pair a new teacher with a "buddy" at the school site with no release time, no common planning time, no compensation, and no professional development. Mentoring is often limited to socioemotional support, guidance in local policies, or technical suggestions for management, rather than reform-minded, standards-based teaching and critical reflection on practice to meet the needs of all learners (Wang & Odell, 2002).

One reason for these problematic practices is a limited conception of new teachers as learners and the goals of induction. The dominant conception throughout the latter part of the 20th century is one of new teacher in the throes of the "survival period," learning to take basic content knowledge and transmit it to well-managed students. This model persists today in the literature and policy rhetoric, is part of the popular conception, and remains largely unquestioned. In this model, novices are reported to experience a form of "practice shock" (Veenman, 1984) as they enter the classroom. The notion of a new teacher "survival phase" (Fuller & Bown, 1975) identifies teachers in a defensive position concerned with student control, administrative review, and making it day to day. Developmental theories identify the phase as one preoccupied with self and a sense of competence. Such theorists find that concerns about self must be addressed before teachers can focus on the needs of students (Huberman, 1993; Kagan, 1992). Along with survival models, other depictions of novices reflect a resurgence of the idea that novices need merely basic subject knowledge, basic pedagogy such as classroom control techniques, and scripted curriculum. (For discussion of how this depiction may contribute to new teacher tracking into lower-order learning contexts, see Achinstein, Ogawa, & Speiglman, 2004.)

Models of mentoring built on the dominant paradigm of novices in survival mode restrict mentors' roles. Just as Bruner (1996) described how 20th-century models of the student as learner guided teachers' decisions (e.g., when we thought of the learner as an empty vessel, the pedagogy was transmission mode), beliefs about the new teacher as learner similarly frame the nature of mentoring. The model that has dominated mentoring is derived from reductive conceptions of novices. If one believes that the new teacher is a survivor in a challenging context, trying to impart basic knowledge to well-managed kids, then mentoring entails helping novices adjust to new environments, learn routines, keep management plans in place, and learn some tips and techniques of teaching. Researchers have documented that all too often, mentoring is focused on situational adjustment, technical advice, emotional support, and local guidance (Feiman-Nemser, 2001; Little, 1990; Wang & Odell, 2002). A humanistic perspective focused on helping novices deal with reality shock through emotional adjustment and self-image support has pervaded the field. A situated apprentice perspective providing technical support in the local context also has been a dominant perspective of mentoring programs (Wang & Odell, 2002). These conceptions identify the purposes of induction as enculturating new teachers into the current system to help novices fit into their new environments, rather than critiquing or challenging existing schooling practices.

Some scholars have challenged these limited models of new teacher learners. Grossman (1990) found that novices are capable of wrestling with complex content-knowledge development in their students; and Gore and Zeichner (1991) criticized how the limited models failed to consider ways new teachers can and should wrestle with ethical and political issues regarding limitations of schooling, rather than learning to replicate the status quo. We review these and other critiques and offer a new one ourselves in Chapter 1 (see also Athanases & Achinstein, 2003). Recent reforms necessitate different norms than those identified in the survival models. These call for teachers to be change agents, reflective practitioners, collaborative colleagues, and lifelong learners—educators who are student-centered, equity-focused, and constructivist. These calls challenge the status quo of teaching and schooling and, therefore, of mentoring.

Limited Models of Mentor Development

Many mentoring situations still fall short of more ideal practices. Often there is little release time or professional support for the work. Within and across induction programs, there is uneven quality among mentors and lack of consensus about mentors' roles and knowledge needed (Feiman-Nemser et al., 1999). A key reason for underdeveloped mentor programs and practices is the belief that new teacher mentors come ready-made. Thus, mentor selection is haphazard and professional development often missing or extremely limited. Furthermore, the professional development that may be provided rests on limited conceptions of the mentor as learner. Much of the relevant literature still tends to provide a technical/manual approach that reduces the mentor to a technician and mentoring to strategies and tips, rather than situating mentoring in complex contexts where issues collide and compete. These practical guides to managing programs and mentors promote a sense of rational technical solutions that reduce uncertainty and eclipse much of the complexity of enacting a role full of tensions. Yet more recent views of professional development and teacher as learner cast educators as reflective practitioners.

These problematic assumptions and practices about new teachers and mentors miss an opportunity to design induction and mentoring that more deeply support work of new teachers and that hold potential to transform the quality of the profession. It is time to articulate more ambitious goals for induction and mentoring, goals that rest on new assumptions about novices as learners and the kinds of knowledge mentors need to support new teachers in the 21st century.

TOWARD NEW CONCEPTIONS
AND PRACTICES IN MENTORING

If one believes the new teacher is not merely in survival mode, but is someone with the ability to focus on individual student learning, to consider content and pedagogy, and to be active in a school's culture, then mentoring entails something much different than emotional and technical support. *Mentors in the Making* contributes to an emerging literature of researchers and educators who have begun to identify an alternative vision of induction and mentoring, based on different assumptions about the new teacher as learner. We challenge the "survival" focus of much of teacher induction. This new stance envisions induction as an opportunity to help new teachers critically reflect on their own practices and schooling in order to foster equitable learning opportunities for all children and to become change agents of the system. It also envisions a reform-minded new teacher engaged in a community of learners. This transformative approach identifies teachers and mentors as collaboratively engaged in a change process that impacts students, themselves, classrooms, organizations, and ultimately the profession. This new vision of mentoring includes several guiding assumptions reflected in this book.

Educative Mentoring and Critical Perspectives

If we hold higher expectations for new teachers as learners and hope to meet ambitious reform goals, then mentoring must move beyond emotional support and brief technical advice to become truly educative, focused on learning opportunities that move novices' practice forward and challenge their thinking and practice (Feiman-Nemser et al., 1999). This kind of mentoring differs from mere affective support, short-term assistance, or occupational socialization, highlighting the critical nature of mentors' focus on cognitive development, where mentors are "cothinkers who engage in productive consultations" (Feiman-Nemser, 2001, p. 22). Mentors can interrupt the survival mode, guiding the new teacher to focus on learners and learning. They can support new teachers to critically "reframe" their thinking about student and classroom challenges, looking through new lenses and reconsidering their own practices and assumptions (Achinstein & Barrett, 2004).

Mentoring can promote a "critical constructivist perspective," supporting novices to teach for social justice and equity (Wang & Odell, 2002). In this approach, mentors are committed to reform-minded teaching and know how to work with novices as agents of change, helping new teachers pose problems of teaching, uncover assumptions, and reconstruct practice (Wang & Odell, 2002). Here the mentor, too, is a change agent, critically reflecting with the novice about classroom and school. In this perspective mentoring moves from traditional knowledge *transmission* to knowledge *transformation*, where mentors work with new teachers to challenge current arrangements in classrooms and schools and to foster reform (Cochran-Smith & Paris, 1995).

Mentor as Learner and Inquirer

A new conception of teacher as learner also requires a new conception of mentor as learner. We know that many induction programs select mentors on the basis of their being lead teachers, veteran teachers of some distinction, or teachers of greatest seniority (e.g., Porter, Youngs, & Odden, 2001). Although they have distinguished themselves in their classrooms, assuming these good teachers make good mentors of new teachers is problematic. Outside the world of teaching, critics often claim that teaching and even mentoring are simple. Such opinions fail to consider current understandings of what effective teachers need to know and be able to do, let alone what it takes to mentor novices. Making mentors needs to be cast as a deliberate act that rests on a knowledge base for effective mentoring. Authors in this book assume that development of mentors is a process and that mentors are thinking educators who reflect on their practice, inquire, and engage in communities of practice with other mentors. Mentors are problem-posers who examine challenges of practice and seek to identify avenues for ongoing learning and growth. Mentors can be facilitators and also collaborators with novices, co-constructing knowledge and learning from the mentoring exchange (Achinstein & Villar, 2004). Thus mentors are not born, but made, and are in a continuing process of becoming.

Mentor as Change Agent and Educational Leader

Mentors provide classroom-based support but also assume leadership in larger contexts. Mentoring with a critical perspective, with mentors and new teachers as agents of change, can foster more equitable teaching and schooling practices. Rather than enculturating novices into the status quo, mentors can promote empowerment and transformation for students, teachers, and schools. Mentors also take on advocacy roles within and across schools and districts, promoting quality working conditions for novices and equitable learning opportunities for students. They build relationships with district and school site administrators, teacher colleagues, unions, parents, and communities. They learn about and transform organizational contexts for novices. Moreover, mentors involved in development of other mentors or who direct induction programs take on additional leadership. If mentors carry a vision of transformative leadership, promoting reform-minded teaching, collaborative decisionmaking, equitable teaching and learning environments, and quality teacher working contexts, they become leaders reshaping the profession.

Mentor Work Shaped by Professional Knowledge Base

While individual mentors can and do engage in highly effective work with new teachers at many sites in the United States and internationally, how can we learn about the deep and often tacit knowledge that guides this work?

In one sense, this argues for a pooling of understandings across many sites. It also argues for carefully analyzing domains of knowledge that undergird these best practices so other new mentors can benefit from this legacy. Mapping a knowledge base also enables a profession to understand its problem areas, dilemmas, and limitations. As educators have developed the knowledge base of teaching, we now face a challenge of articulating another knowledge base for the profession. We need a better understanding of what mentors need to know and be able to do to effectively guide work of new teachers of the 21st century. Developing a knowledge base for mentors of necessity borrows from teaching and other professions in which a professional knowledge base and standards are grounded in work of their practitioners.

TOWARD A KNOWLEDGE BASE
OF EFFECTIVE MENTORING

By knowledge base, we mean a "codified or codifiable aggregation" of knowledge, understanding, skill, and disposition (Shulman, 1987, p. 4). This includes things we imagine "in the brain" but also includes skill (the ability to enact knowledge) and disposition (a propensity to act or not act on what one knows). A knowledge base for teaching categorizes knowledge and provides "a means of representing and communicating it" (Shulman, 1987, p. 4). For practitioner knowledge to become a professional knowledge base, it must be public, represented in a form enabling its cumulative and shared nature, and continually verified and improved (Hiebert, Gallimore, & Stigler, 2002). The teaching profession has seen this *improving* of collective professional understandings (what Shulman called the "ever-growing" knowledge base).

To develop an understanding of the complexity of a mentor's knowledge, we build on models of teacher knowledge developed by Shulman (1987), Wilson, Shulman, and Richert (1987), Grossman (1990), Grimmett and MacKinnon (1992), and Ladson-Billings (2001). Drawing on this literature and several assessment projects, Darling-Hammond et al. (1999) divided the knowledge base into three broad domains of knowledge that we use to organize the mentoring knowledge base and to structure the parts of this book: (1) learners and learning, (2) curriculum and teaching, and (3) contexts and purposes.

However, Figure I.1 shows how mentors' knowledge must operate at two levels: focused on both students and teachers. Across knowledge domains, the bottom row of the table marks how targeting students rests at the foundation. However, the upper row, targeting teachers, shows how effective mentors also use nuanced approaches to addressing needs of the adult learner

Figure I.1. The Bilevel Nature of the Knowledge Base for Mentoring

	Learners and Learning	Curriculum and Teaching	Contexts and Purposes
Targeting New Teachers	Novice as adult learner Novice development and needs Novice knowledge base, strategies, and cultural competence Novice's reflectivity level and receptivity to change	Professional knowledge: content, standards, assessment Knowledge of guiding educational reform and inquiry Pedagogies of mentoring Roles and interactional stances Languages of mentoring	Embedded professional contexts and communities Organizational and political literacy Leadership and change agency Philosophies of induction
Targeting Students	Students as learners, individuals, and group members Learning theory Cultural competence Pedagogical learner knowledge	General pedagogical knowledge Content knowledge Pedagogical content knowledge Reform-focused and culturally responsive teaching Content standards and assessment	Schools and society Social and political contexts Classroom and community contexts that shape learning Educational philosophies

in context. To enact a bilevel knowledge base, the mentor assumes a *bifocal perspective* on teachers and students. Up close, the mentor focuses on the new teacher, what she or he knows and needs. The mentor simultaneously holds the big picture in view, which is the students, their learning, and their needs. The bifocal perspective makes mentoring especially complex, as mentors must at times face conflicts in meeting the needs of both student and adult learners. For example, to address inequitable learning opportunities that a language-minority student experiences in class means confronting the adult learner about her or his practices while still trying to build a trusting relationship with the novice. Since the bottom row (targeting students) is likely more familiar to readers, we only briefly highlight a few concepts there. The upper row (targeting teachers) organizes concepts explored in this book. This figure represents our current best understanding of the mentor's knowledge base, drawing on research and practice in the book chapters and informed by other researchers' work.

Mentor Knowledge Domains Targeting Students

The figure shows that knowledge of *learners and learning* targeted at students involves areas often explored in teacher education. We highlight, however, two concepts at the bottom of this cell of the table. First, cultural competence includes understandings of culture and students' communities, the role of culture in education and as a basis for student learning. It also involves the teachers' broader knowledge of sociopolitical issues related to racism, linguicism, and white privilege and a commitment to focusing on equity (Ladson-Billings, 2001). Second, pedagogical learner knowledge (Grimmett & MacKinnon, 1992) is how knowledge of particular learners from different cultural, social, and family backgrounds can inform pedagogical decisions.

Curriculum and teaching targeted at students requires general pedagogical knowledge, or a broad knowledge of principles and techniques of teaching, as well as content knowledge steeped in subject matter domains and forms of reasoning within a discipline. This domain also identifies pedagogical content knowledge (Shulman, 1987), which includes knowledge of how to structure and sequence subject matter in meaningful ways and how to scaffold content to make it accessible to students. Reform-minded and culturally responsive practices that reflect teaching for understanding and meeting the needs of diverse learners are also central to this domain.

Knowledge of *contexts and purposes* targeted at students involves knowledge of relationships between schools and society and of the larger social and political contexts in which schools are embedded. Furthermore, mentors need to know about classroom and local community contexts that influence student learning, including students' neighborhoods and home cultures. This same cell also highlights knowledge of diverse educational philosophies and larger purposes of schooling in a democracy.

Mentor Knowledge Domains Targeting Teachers

Figure I.1 shows how knowledge of *learners and learning* targeted at new teachers involves knowledge about adult learners and working with novices. It highlights mentors' knowledge of a novice's learning style, values, and vision, as well as understandings of novice development, needs, and concerns. This requires knowing teachers as individuals and as members of cultural groups with prior experiences that they bring to teaching. Mentors need to be aware of the kinds of demands on novices as they learn to teach.

It includes assessing the new teachers' knowledge base and repertoire of teaching strategies. Mentors need to address novices' cultural competence, attitudes about, awareness of, and commitments to diverse students. Further, this includes assessing novices' reflectivity level, openness to mentoring, and receptivity to change.

Curriculum and teaching targeted at new teachers includes mentors' knowledge of professional teaching standards novices are expected to master, how to teach deep content knowledge to novices, and how to provide formative assessment of teaching practice to tailor support and guide novice development. Figure I.1 shows mentors' capacity to guide novices' development of reform-focused teaching and schooling. They need to know how to systematically inquire about and reflect on novices' practice, as well as engage novices in reflection and inquiry about beliefs, practices, and outcomes of their teaching. This domain highlights pedagogies of mentoring such as: observation and analysis strategies; collaborative lesson and unit planning; analysis of student work; and working with novices to set goals and develop individualized learning plans to meet those goals. Furthermore, it includes mentoring roles and interactional stances that extend new teachers' thinking. Such stances range from instructional (where the mentor guides and introduces new knowledge), to more collaborative (where mentor and novice co-construct knowledge), to facilitative exchanges (where the new teacher moves to more autonomous thinking). Mentors need to both pace (listen to the new teacher to understand his or her concerns) and lead (hold higher outcomes and a focused direction in mind for the mentoring exchanges). Finally, knowledge of mentoring languages involves discourse tactics that build trust through nonjudgmental exchanges, while extending novices' development through a repertoire of questioning, suggestion, and instructional skills.

Knowledge of *contexts and purposes* targeted at new teachers requires knowledge of multiple embedded professional contexts that shape teachers' work lives (McLaughlin & Talbert, 2001). Each context promotes certain norms, practices, and expectations that inform mentors' work. Starting from the outside environments and moving inward, such contexts include: federal, state, district, and school governance and policy systems; local and larger political climate; educational professional environments; induction programs; school organization, culture, politics, programs, resources, and policies; administrators; teacher community and culture; parent community and student population. Figure I.1 also shows political literacy (Kelchtermans & Ballet, 2003), or the mentors' ability to read how the system works, to navigate and help novices navigate conflicts within that context, and to change the system when it fails to meet the needs of teachers, students, or community. This domain also highlights leadership skills in fostering educational change, particularly for those mentors who move beyond mentoring to direct induction programs. Mentors need knowledge of how to be an agent of change and understand reform processes. Finally, this domain includes knowledge of philosophies of induction and understandings about the multiple and sometimes conflicting purposes of teacher socialization (e.g., to both support novices' entry into the profession and to promote new norms and practices, thus transforming the profession).

While Figure I.1 displays three distinct domains of knowledge and two levels of actors the mentor's work targets, elements of the domains and target groups at times overlap and intersect. For example, pedagogical learner knowledge is an amalgam of learners and curriculum and teaching. A thoughtful teacher considers pedagogical decisions based on prior knowledge, experiences, and needs of individual learners. Similarly, learners are best understood within their organizational contexts (e.g., teacher concerns are specific to particular professional contexts in which they work). Further, while a mentor targets two levels, teachers and students, the levels intersect when a mentor considers a specific teacher's needs in relation to her or his specific student population. Thus, while the figure highlights differences in domains and target groups, knowledge that mentors need is more fluid and connects concepts across domains and levels.

ABOUT THE BOOK

Clearly, teacher induction and mentoring need new visions, development of an informing knowledge base about effective mentoring, and structures to enable such work to occur. Central to the work must be leaders who emerge as both mentors and organizers of induction activities, leaders who face challenges unforeseen in a profession that barely recognized the need for induction a mere 15 years ago. To develop new conceptions of mentoring, and to understand dilemmas faced in practice, we sought out innovative, carefully conceptualized, well-developed induction programs, case studies of mentoring, and the expertise of educators and researchers to provide us with images of the possible.

Learning Among a Network of Induction Leaders

This book highlights in particular the work of an unusual educational network. Participants in some of the studies and authors of several chapters have been members of an educational reform network of induction leaders that includes collaborating researchers. The Leadership Network for Teacher

Induction (LNTI) includes induction program directors, mentors, university-based researchers, and teacher educators who have engaged deeply in the work of induction in Northern California for three years. California had a statewide-funded program of beginning teacher support and assessment. Through an ongoing collaboration over three years, the Network, supported by the New Teacher Center at the University of California, Santa Cruz, has fostered innovative work that pushes the boundaries of knowledge about induction through systematic inquiry into mentoring and program development in the greater San Francisco Bay area of California.

LNTI members serve as a rich source for exploring a knowledge base and the complexities of mentoring new teachers. First, LNTI members have had a wealth of experience as teachers, mentors, mentor leaders, and induction program developers. Second, LNTI members have reflected on and conducted action research as part of LNTI work to investigate and improve on problem areas in their teacher induction work. Third, in ongoing sessions, LNTI members have engaged in reflective conversations with other leaders who represent programs from over 60 districts in Northern California. These programs have supported the work of a total of 2,750 new teachers and 772 mentors. These districts vary from lower-income, large urban districts serving almost exclusively students of color, to smaller, more affluent suburban districts in predominantly white communities. Having members of far-ranging and diverse districts present has supported the search for both similarities and differences in discussions of what teacher induction means, what mentoring can yield, and how problems of teacher induction can be identified and addressed. Finally, LNTI has provided a forum for participants to create an ongoing learning community that uses mutual knowledge, learning, and collaboration to explore critical issues in education, rather than relying solely on transmission of outsider knowledge—features of many successful education networks (Lieberman & Grolnick, 1996). In this way, LNTI members have worked in a network that supports, taps, and develops their expertise of practice and knowledge grounded in inquiry. We have been active participants in this Network as co-facilitator of the Network (Betty) and collaborator in the action research writing process (Steven).

In our research with this community of induction leaders we began to map the knowledge base of mentoring and to identify evidence of this knowledge base in practice. We found parallels with the knowledge base of teaching that highlighted the three major domains of knowledge (Figure I.1) that serve to organize this book. While we mapped this knowledge base, several areas arose as particularly problematic. Some of the challenging areas represent departures from the knowledge base of teaching. Others remain missing foci and areas of concern. The book examines these challenging areas explicitly.

Organization

In Part I we begin by highlighting the challenge of focusing novices on the needs of diverse learners. The chapters in this part ask: How can mentors' knowledge of formative assessment target new teachers' attention to individual and low-performing students? What knowledge is needed for mentors to focus new teachers on issues of diversity and equity? How can mentor professional development make equity explicit?

Part II focuses on what mentors should know and be able to do in relation to curriculum and teaching. The chapters identify challenges in developing and enacting a knowledge base of curriculum and teaching for mentors, including: mentoring stances, subject-matter–specific mentoring, locally tailored mentor development, and curricula for mentor learning.

What do mentors need to know and be able to act upon in relation to organizational contexts and purposes of induction? This question is addressed in Part III. The chapters highlight challenges and promising practices in mentors' organizational knowledge in two areas: (1) navigating and transforming organizational politics; and (2) induction program leadership. The authors also address how mentors and mentor leaders articulate purposes of induction, exposing underlying values about socialization and transformation embedded in their work.

Our conclusion points toward future directions for practice, policy, and research in mentoring and induction.

NOTE

1. For example, Smith and Ingersoll (2004) found that having a mentor in the same field as the novice reduced the risk of a teacher leaving the profession after the first year by 30%. Strong and St. John (2001) reported retention rates from a comprehensive mentoring program, finding that 89% remained in the classroom and 94% remained in education after 6 years. Fletcher, Strong, and Villar (2004) demonstrated that classes of novices supported by a comprehensive mentoring program showed achievement gains similar to those students in classes taught by more experienced teachers.

REFERENCES

Achinstein, B., & Barrett, A. (2004). (Re)framing classroom contexts: How new teachers and mentors view diverse learners and challenges of practice. *Teachers College Record, 106*(4), 716–746.

Achinstein, B., Ogawa, R., & Speiglman, A. (2004). Are we creating separate and unequal tracks of teachers? The impact of state policy, local conditions, and teacher background on new teacher socialization. *American Educational Research Journal, 41*(3), 557–603.

Achinstein, B., & Villar, A. (2004). A spectrum of mentoring relationships and new teacher learning: Collaboration and complexity. *Journal of Educational Change, 5*(4), 311–344.

Athanases, S. Z., & Achinstein, B. (2003). Focusing new teachers on individual and low performing students: The centrality of formative assessment in the mentor's repertoire of practice. *Teachers College Record, 105*(8), 1486–1520.

Ballantyne, R., Hansford, B., & Packer, J. (1995). Mentoring beginning teachers: A qualitative analysis of process and outcomes. *Educational Review, 47*(3), 297–307.

Britton, E., Paine, L., Pimm, D., & Raizen, S. (2003). *Comprehensive teacher induction: Systems for early career learning.* Dordrecht, Netherlands, and San Francisco: Kluwer & WestEd.

Bruner, J. (1996). *The culture of education.* Cambridge, MA: Harvard University Press.

Bush, R. N. (1983). *The beginning years of teaching: A focus for collaboration in teacher education.* Paper presented to the World Assembly of the International Council on Education for Teachers, Washington, DC.

California Department of Education. (2003). *Personnel Assignment Information Form (PAIF) 2002–03.* Sacramento: Author.

Cochran-Smith, M., & Paris, P. (1995). Mentor and mentoring: Did Homer have it right? In J. Smith (Ed.), *Critical discourses on teacher development* (pp. 181–202). London: Cassell.

Darling-Hammond, L. (1997). *Doing what matters most: Investing in quality teaching.* New York: National Commission on Teaching and America's Future.

Darling-Hammond, L., Wise, A. E., & Klein, S. P. (1999). *A license to teach: Raising standards for teaching.* San Francisco: Jossey-Bass.

Feiman-Nemser, S. (2001). Helping novices learn to teach: Lessons from an exemplary support teacher. *Journal of Teacher Education, 52*(1), 17–30.

Feiman-Nemser, S., Schwille, S., Carver, C., & Yusko, B. (1999). *A conceptual review of literature on new teacher induction.* A work product of the National Partnership on Excellence and Accountability in Education Report. Washington, DC: U.S. Department of Education.

Fletcher, S., Strong, M., & Villar, A. (2004). *An investigation of the effects of teacher experience and teacher preparedness on the performance of Latino students in California.* Santa Cruz: The New Teacher Center, University of California, Santa Cruz.

Fuller, F. F., & Bown, O. H. (1975). Becoming a teacher. In K. Ryan (Ed), *Teacher education* (74th Yearbook of the National Society for the Study of Education, pp. 25–52). Chicago: The University of Chicago Press.

Gore, J. M., & Zeichner, K. M. (1991). Action research and reflective teaching in preservice teacher education: A case study from the United States. *Teaching and Teacher Education, 7,* 119–136.

Grimmett, P., & Mackinnon, A. (1992). Craft knowledge and the education of teachers. In G. Grant (Ed.), *Review of research in education* (pp. 385–456). Washington, DC: American Educational Research Association.

Grossman, P. (1990). *The making of a teacher: Teacher knowledge and teacher education.* New York: Teachers College Press.

Hanushek, E. (1992). The trade-off between child quantity and quality. *Journal of Political Economy, 100*(1), 84–117.

Hiebert, J., Gallimore, R., & Stigler, J. W. (2002). A knowledge base for the teaching profession: What would it look like and how can we get one? *Educational Researcher, 31*(5), 3–15.

Huberman, M. (1993). *The lives of teachers.* New York: Teachers College Press.

Huling-Austin, L. (1990). Teacher induction programs and internships. In W. R. Houston, M. Haberman, & J. Sikula (Eds.), *Handbook of research on teacher education* (pp. 535–548). New York: Macmillan.

Ingersoll, R. M. (2001a). *A different approach to solving the teacher shortage problem* (Teacher Quality Policy Brief Number 3). Seattle, WA: Center for the Study of Teaching and Policy, University of Washington.

Ingersoll, R. M. (2001b). Teacher turnover and teacher shortages: An organizational analysis. *American Educational Research Journal, 38*(3), 499–534.

Ingersoll, R. M. (2002). The teacher shortage: A case of wrong diagnosis and wrong prescription. *NASSP Bulletin, 86*, 16–31.

Ingersoll, R. M., & Smith, T. (2003a, April). *Reducing teacher turnover: What are the components of effective induction?* Paper presented at the annual meeting of the American Educational Research Association, Chicago.

Ingersoll, R. M., & Smith, T. (2003b). The wrong solution to the teacher shortage. *Educational Leadership, 60*(8), 30–33.

Johnson, S. M. (2004). *Finders and keepers: Helping new teachers survive and thrive in our schools.* San Francisco: Jossey-Bass.

Kagan, D. M. (1992). Professional growth among preservice and beginning teachers. *Review of Educational Research, 62*(2), 129–169.

Kelchtermans, G., & Ballet, K. (2003). Micropolitical literacy: Reconstructing a neglected dimension in teacher development. *International Journal of Educational Research, 37*, 755–767.

Ladson-Billings, G. (2001). *Crossing over to Canaan: The journey of new teachers in diverse classrooms.* San Francisco: Jossey-Bass.

Lieberman, A., & Grolnick, M. (1996). Networks and reform in American education. *Teachers College Record, 98*(1), 7–45.

Little, J. W. (1990). The mentor phenomenon and the social organization of teaching. In C. B. Cazden (Ed.), *Review of Research in Education, Vol. 16* (pp. 297–351). Washington, DC: American Educational Research Association.

McLaughlin, M., & Talbert, J. E. (2001). *Professional communities and the work of high school teaching.* Chicago: University of Chicago Press.

Murnane, R., Singer, J., Willet, J., Kemple, J., & Olsen, R. (Eds.). (1991). *Who will teach? Policies that matter.* Cambridge, MA: Harvard University Press.

National Commission on Teaching and America's Future [NCTAF]. (1996). *What matters most: Teaching for America's future.* New York: Author.

Odell, S. J., & Ferraro, D. P. (1992). Teacher mentoring and teacher retention. *Journal of Teacher Education, 43*(3), 200–204.

Orland, L. (2001). Reading a mentoring situation: One aspect of learning to mentor. *Teaching and Teacher Education, 17*(1), 75–88.

Pearson, M. J. T., & Honig, B. (1992). *Success for beginning teachers: The California New Teacher Project.* Sacramento: Commission on Teacher Credentialing.

Porter, A., Youngs, P., & Odden, A. (2001). Advances in teacher assessments and
their uses. In V. Richardson (Ed.), *Handbook of research on teaching* (4th ed.,
pp. 259–297). Washington, DC: American Educational Research Association.

Quality counts. (2003). *http://www.edweek.org/sreports/qc03/reports/17support-
t1.cfm.*

Rivkin, S. G., Hanushek, E. A., & Kain, J. F. (2005). Teachers, schools, and academic achievement. *Econometrics, 73*(2), 417–458.

Sanders, W., & Rivers, J. (1996). *Cumulative and residual effects of teachers on
future academic achievement.* Knoxville, TN: University of Tennessee Value-
Added Research and Assessment Center.

Schlechty, P., & Vance, V. (1983). Recruitment, selection and retention: The shape
of the teaching force. *Elementary School Journal, 83*(4), 469–487.

Shields, P. M., Humphrey, D. C., Wechsler, M. E., Riehl, L. M., Tiffany-Morales,
J., Woodworth, K., et. al. (2001). *Teaching and California's future: The status
of the teaching profession 2001.* Santa Cruz, CA: The Center for the Future of
Teaching and Learning.

Shulman, L. S. (1987). Knowledge and teaching: Foundations of the new reform.
Harvard Educational Review, 57(1), 1–22.

Smith, T. M., & Ingersoll, R. M. (2004). What are the effects of induction and
mentoring on beginning teacher turnover? *American Educational Research
Journal, 41*(3), 681–714.

Strong, M., & St. John, L. (2001). *A study of teacher retention: The effects of
mentoring for beginning teachers.* Santa Cruz: The New Teacher Center, University of California Santa Cruz.

Veenman, S. (1984). Perceived problems of beginning teachers. *Review of Educational Research, 54*(2), 143–178.

Wang, J., & Odell, S. J. (2002). Mentored learning to teach according to standards-
based reform: A critical review. *Review of Educational Research, 72*(3), 481–
546.

Wilson, S. M., Darling-Hammond, L., & Berry, B. (2001). *A case of successful teaching policy: Connecticut's long-term efforts to improve teaching and learning.*
Seattle, WA: Center for the Study of Teaching and Policy.

Wilson, S. M., Shulman, L. S., & Richert, A. E. (1987). 150 different ways of knowing: Representations of knowledge in teaching. In J. Calderhead (Ed.), *Exploring teachers' thinking* (pp. 104–124). Sussex, England: Holt, Rinehart, and
Winston.

PART I

A Mentor's Knowledge of Learners and Learning

The chapters in this part ask: What do mentors need to know about the learning of both student and teacher learners? They highlight a particular challenge in the domain of learner knowledge—that of focusing novices on the needs of culturally and linguistically diverse learners and supporting teachers in addressing issues of equity.

In Chapter 1, Athanases and Achinstein address what mentors need to know and be able to do to focus new teachers on individual student learning, particularly of low-performing students, and what the complexities of this knowledge base are as enacted in the mentoring process. This chapter builds on models of teacher knowledge and finds that central to mentors' knowledge base is a range of assessment strategies, including assessment of students, alignment of teaching with standards, and formative assessment of the teacher. Skillful use of that knowledge in mentoring conversations can bring individual student learning into focus and provide new teachers with methods to shape instruction to meet students' varied learning needs.

In Chapter 2, Achinstein and Athanases report on an investigation of what mentors need to know and be able to do to guide new teachers to meet the needs of their culturally and linguistically diverse students, with particular attention to educational equity. They found that mentors need a *bifocal perspective* on teachers and students, and pedagogical learner knowledge (Grimmett & MacKinnon, 1992) that allows teachers to understand learners from different cultural backgrounds, properly interpret their understandings, and support their development. Using a case study, the chapter also examines how problematic this mentoring can be in process, even when the mentor has strong convictions and substantive preparation.

In Chapter 3, Enid Lee focuses on building mentors' capacity to make equity explicit and to mentor from an antiracist perspective. She highlights equity challenges that mentors identify in their work, describes key elements of a professional development series targeted at addressing these concerns, and provides recommendations for moving mentors and new teachers toward racial equality in teacher induction and student achievement.

REFERENCE

Grimmett, P., & Mackinnon, A. (1992). Craft knowledge and the education of teachers. In G. Grant (Ed.), *Review of research in education* (pp. 385–456). Washington, DC: American Educational Research Association.

CHAPTER 1

Mentors' Knowledge of Formative Assessment: Guiding New Teachers to Look Closely at Individual Students

Steven Z. Athanases and Betty Achinstein

> Beginning teachers have a tough time with assessment; they are so focused on themselves and what they are doing each day that they can't get much beyond that. They are in "survival mode."

This mentor articulates the popular view that new teachers focus on self-image, resources, and procedures. Though grounded in research reviews and professional lore, this view mistakenly assumes that teachers move through predictable stages from a focus on self, to curriculum, and finally, after some time, to student academic learning (Bullough, 1997; Grossman, 1992; Richardson & Placier, 2001). This view also ignores possibilities of educative mentoring (Feiman-Nemser, 2001). Little work has examined how mentors can help new teachers move past survival mode to focus on individual student learning. A study we conducted addressed these concerns, challenging the limited developmental models of teaching.

Mentors in the Making: Developing New Leaders for New Teachers, edited by Betty Achinstein and Steven Z. Athanases. Copyright © 2006 by Teachers College, Columbia University. All rights reserved. Prior to photocopying items for classroom use, please contact the Copyright Clearance Center, Customer Service, 222 Rosewood Dr., Danvers, MA 01923, USA, tel. (978) 750-8400.

THE POTENTIAL OF MENTORING TO FOCUS
NEW TEACHERS ON LEARNERS

Some early evidence suggests that mentoring has helped new teachers move beyond classroom management concerns to a focus on individual students' learning (Darling-Hammond, Gendler, & Wise, 1990; Huling-Austin, 1989). Many induction programs use relevant practices, including ways to track learning of target students, review student work, and use formative assessment. Programs also often link to professional standards for teaching and learning that focus novices on understanding student differences, engaging all learners, and planning lessons tailored to diverse learners.[1]

Despite this promise, contexts constrain mentoring practice. In programs in the United States, the United Kingdom, and China, for example, although mentors claim a focus on individual students as central to their mentoring, little mentor–novice time explores such concerns, with far more time spent learning to adhere to local norms (Wang, 2001). Tapped for their seniority, mentors often act as local guides, uninformed by clear conceptions of effective mentoring.

Recently, a knowledge base has been emerging related to ways a mentor can focus on individual learners (e.g., Feiman-Nemser, 2001; Kilbourn & Roberts, 1991; Orland, 2001). Our study contributes by asking: (1) What do mentors need to know and be able to do to focus new teachers on individual student learning? (2) What are the complexities of this knowledge base as enacted in the mentoring process? To address the first question, we explored knowledge of the Leadership Network for Teacher Induction (LNTI, see Introduction). We used questionnaires in which participants identified and selectively illustrated the three most important things mentors need to know and be able to do to help new teachers focus on individual student learning. LNTI members in this study included 37 teacher induction leaders, mostly but not exclusively white women.

We also wanted to know what this knowledge base looked like in action, so we examined cases of mentoring from a 2-year study. The study included 20 beginning teacher–mentor pairs in an intensive Northern California induction program of one of the LNTI teams. We examined two cases closely because they highlighted themes emerging from the questionnaire. Also, the cases raised questions and revealed complexities. The featured cases involved two mentor–novice pairs in the same highly regarded, inquiry-oriented induction program. Mentors were rigorously selected and extensively trained. Novices received 2 years of weekly mentor support and monthly seminars.

Informed by research on the knowledge base for teaching (Feiman-Nemser & Remillard, 1996; Grossman, 1990; Shulman, 1987), we examined questionnaires and developed categories that reflected mentors' conceptions. We then examined transcripts of case study mentoring conversations and interviews for evidence of themes from our questionnaire analyses and derived new categories from the cases. (For discussion of the full study, see Athanases & Achinstein, 2003.)

DOMAINS OF ASSESSMENT IN THE MENTOR'S REPERTOIRE

The dominant theme, cited by nearly all participants from the induction leaders network, was that mentors need to develop complex knowledge in three domains of assessment in order to help new teachers focus on individual student learning.

Basic Knowledge of Assessment of Students

Participants reported that mentors need knowledge of a wide range of student assessment tools and practices to help new teachers develop these. This included multiple measures, since, as one noted, "one type of assessment does not reveal all learnings." Participants wrote of the need to know formal and informal strategies, ability to track growth over time, necessary evidence to collect, and how to assess learning during instruction. Another key theme was the ability to examine student work carefully. The mentor needs to know how to examine assessment results, how to analyze student data, and how to use rubrics judiciously. Such work can yield at least two distinct classroom results. The first is helping the new teacher know "how to accurately assess students' levels of development in relation to criteria, then articulate what the student(s) know/don't know." The second involves the formative component of using this knowledge for "individualized and differentiated instruction."

Knowledge of Standards and How to Gauge Curricular Alignment

The second domain of assessment knowledge mentors need, according to respondents, is a command of subject matter and grade-level standards for student performance and knowledge of how to align these with curriculum. This enables the mentor to help the novice align practice with both state- and district-level standards. Mentors also need to know standards for teacher performance, to know when expectations for performance need to be met.

Knowledge of Formative Assessment of Beginning Teachers

The third and most prominent domain of assessment knowledge concerned formative assessment of the new teacher. This involves enacting the role of assessor of the new teacher's student learning focus. Remarks pointed to three elements in this domain.

Observe and assess new teacher's focus on learners. Mentors need to gauge novices' knowledge of their students. This includes academic information such as class performance and test scores, home and family life, personal learning styles and needs, and academic and social place in the larger group. Another area is classroom interaction patterns, especially how the teacher "interacts with the class as a whole, and with individual students." One respondent asked, "How is the beginning teacher engaging the students? Does the mentor have enough information to help in this area? What strategies? Content knowledge?" The mentor also needs to assess effectiveness of the new teacher's instructional strategies and assessment methods: how the teacher develops assessments, how student work aligns with expectations, what is done with results, and how assessment is used to plan a next lesson. Finally, the mentor needs to collect data to prompt reflective conversation with the teacher, including "scripting" of classroom episodes and observation notes on focal students. Of particular importance is "framing evidence so that beginning teachers can analyze."

Structure learning-focused conversation with the teacher. With data, the mentor can use conversation to present evidence, prompt reflective discussion, listen to teacher thinking, and move a teacher's attention into inquiry about students and their needs. One respondent summarized: "Be able to scaffold a reflective experience and use a variety of techniques such as video, observations, self-observations, and action research." Video can support the mentor's challenge of conveying observations about a teacher's need for better monitoring of student performance: "Often, the video recording, viewed alone or collaboratively, says it all. The beginning teacher 'gets it' and the mentor can proceed to support the next steps."

Guide new teacher growth toward student learning goals. According to respondents, focusing novices on student learning includes a proactive, tutoring function. This includes guiding a new teacher in examining student work. One participant described guiding a small group of teachers to use a teacher-created grade-level writing rubric to evaluate student work. Several induction leaders reported that with careful review of students' work, assessment can guide next-steps instruction to meet all students' needs. One participant recalled encouraging a teacher to ask students to say in writing what they had learned after each lesson and to use results to guide future instruction. Another described reviewing student work with a new teacher: "We found that several students did not reach her goal of expectation, but many did. We worked on a plan together for intervention strategies using different tools to work with the small group."

Novices need support to understand how assessment can be more than summative for final grades, that it can inform understanding of ongoing student learning to shape instruction. Mentors can help novices see assessment in a different light:

> Most of the students of a high school math beginning teacher were failing algebra quizzes. She continued with her predetermined lesson plan despite the fact that 82% of her students did not understand concepts necessary for further understanding. Analyzing the data changed her approach and lesson plans.

Using student data in this way enables an intervention to occur, in part because evidence is seen as more "objective" than something stated by the mentor.

Induction leaders consistently reported that a mentor needs to know relevant student performance standards as benchmarks for work with novices. One noted, "In analyzing student work, I have walked beginning teachers through content standards for language arts. We have looked at student essays in relation to preselected standards and discussed next steps." Another, however, also reported a need to guide new teachers to develop their own understandings of student needs beyond standards. This included asking a novice, "Now that you know what your students' needs are, what do you do next so that the students continue to grow, even though what they need is not addressed in the 'standard' grade-level curriculum?"

ASSESSMENT KNOWLEDGE IN CASES
OF MENTORING PRACTICE

The cases we examined illustrated the power and complexity of a mentor's knowledge of multiple domains of assessment. They show mentors using their knowledge to prompt reflection on individual students and to guide teacher growth toward student learning goals. They also expose challenges and conflicting demands of mentoring.

Using Mentoring Conversations

New teachers need help viewing their classrooms and focusing on students' needs. In conversations, mentors can provide lenses for novices to view students as individuals with varied learning needs and can shine a light on low-performing students. Following are excerpts from planning conferences where a novice shared ideas for a lesson and the mentor prompted thinking and provided feedback. These conferences were held the day before a lesson would be taught, so there was some urgency to design a workable and complete plan. Excerpts also are drawn from reflecting conferences after a lesson was observed. These sessions offered opportunity to examine observational data and student work, to reflect on successes and challenges, and to plan next steps. Examples show the mentor turning a teacher's attention away from solely teacher moves to students, particularly low performers.

Joshua and Meg in conversation. Joshua[2] was a first-year 6th-grade teacher at a K–6 school of 564 students in a midsized city with a racially and linguistically diverse student population. Joshua's mentor, Meg, was a veteran upper elementary grade teacher and an experienced and full-time released mentor. (M = Mentor; T = Teacher.)

M: What about kids like your English language learners, like Jésus, and kids that have some special needs? How are you going to make sure that they have gotten it, that they have success?

T: After they've started the assignment, checking their progress to see that they understand it. . . . Periodically before the day that it's due, looking at their work and seeing what they've done . . . You can ask some questions to see if they understand what's expected. If there is some disconnect, you need to work with them.

M: I know your groups are six or seven. Have you had times when you've had the students work in a partnership when they've gone away to do something like this? They do their own work and have their own product, but they work through the text together . . . What might that look like? Could that give students like Jésus some support?

Joshua then identified partnering practices he had used in the past and articulated the importance of peer scaffolding. Meg used questions to promote further thinking about assessing students' levels and appropriate partnering strategies. The exchange on grouping practices based on student needs helped Joshua see how students with different language and learning needs require different levels and kinds of scaffolding, and that peer grouping practices matter. Meg ended the exchange by bringing the discussion back to the target student, Jésus, identifying how such approaches would support him and other English language learners (ELLs).

In a reflecting conference after the lesson, Meg shared a student participation chart and script of teacher–student exchanges. Joshua used these to describe variance in students' levels of participation in discussion. Meg then focused him on students not involved:

> Have you thought about having some way that levels the playing field so that everyone has equal participation in the group? So that Esme and Jesse aren't dominating? Perhaps you've got these kids who aren't quite as strong, who are a little bit intimidated.

The two then explored strategies to increase equity of participation. One strategy Meg proposed was a ticket system. Groups and individual students are assigned a specific number of tickets, and they must spend those and *only* those during an activity; reticent speakers must contribute, and those who normally dominate must make contributions wisely.

In these exchanges Meg asked, "How are you going to make sure that they have success?" This focused Joshua's attention on his responsibility to address lower-performing or special-needs students. By asking what kind of thinking Joshua could do, Meg foregrounded reflection and inquiry without resolving the issue with her own immediate solution. Further, she solicited what Joshua already did and knew about the students that might work best. By exploring student partnering and grouping strategies, the two examined ways to support ELLs such as Jésus. They also uncovered the complexity of different students' abilities and needs that require varied grouping strategies, sometimes more heterogeneous, sometimes homogeneous. In the reflecting conference, observation data and participation charts pointed out students not engaged. Meg used reflective questions and indirect suggestions to explore alternatives, honoring Joshua's decisionmaking authority, respecting that he knew his classroom context best.

Nan and Lisette in conversation. The second case pair was Nan and her mentor, Lisette. Nan was a first-year 3rd-grade teacher at a K–5 school in a midsized city with a high Latino and migrant population. Lisette was an experienced full-time released mentor who had taught primary grades. Lisette also explicitly focused the new teacher's attention on the needs of low performers in her class of predominantly ELLs. Nan identified Miguel as "the most limited English in proficiency out of all my students," and Julie, who had a learning disability. Lisette recalled Nan's lesson and its fit for these students, asking if "they might be more successful if they had a poem that was a little bit shorter." Nan responded, "That's a good idea. I hadn't thought about that." The mentor's focus was cursory, and she quickly transitioned from student issues to a concern Nan had identified, what to do with students who finish early.

After the lesson, the two target students were briefly addressed again:

> M: How successful did you feel your students were with reading? . . . Some of your goals were that they really worked on fluency, and one of your concerns I remember was would the poems be at the appropriate level? And would you be able to reach all the students and give them good opportunities? So how did you feel about that?
>
> T: For the most part I felt that the selection and the material that I had was appropriate for them. The only person that I would make an exception would be Julie, who . . . could have a learning disability. I noticed that during the lesson she was having a hard time grasping the material that I had selected.
>
> M: Mhmm. But for the most part, you felt like everyone was at least making attempts and able to read their material.

Lisette quickly moved past a focus on Julie's needs to an assessment of Nan's feelings about the group as a whole. Soon they moved on to analyze observation data the mentor had scripted. This led to a brief conversation about Miguel. The teacher noted, "As I looked at the data I see how Miguel takes a lot of my attention and time consistently." Lisette responded:

> M: We had talked about Miguel a little bit before this, so I would think that it might be affirming for you to see this much data that maybe it's time to put Miguel on a contract as we had discussed. How are you feeling about that now? Is that something you think you want to do?
>
> T: Definitely.
>
> M: That's something that we already talked about. So we'll go ahead and put Miguel on a contract. I'll get you some different samples, and you can select which one you'd like.

The new teacher has identified Miguel, a second-language learner, and Julie, a learning-disabled student, as challenges she wanted to discuss with Lisette. In the planning conference the mentor briefly explored these, suggesting adjusting materials and assignment to meet these students' needs, then quickly moved on to the next concern of the teacher's. In the reflecting conference, Lisette asked Nan about her students' success in reading and if she was able to reach all students. She solicited Nan's perception of how that felt. Nan still identified Julie as a challenge. Yet Lisette jumped past that comment with a feelings-oriented focus on only the full class. While she could have deeply engaged these moments to examine different needs of ELLs and learning-disabled students, or addressed unique needs of the two separate individuals, or raised questions for Nan about her ideas for how to address their needs, instead she provided rapid solutions of shortening poems that they would read and of placing Miguel on a contract. While these choices are understandable given immediate needs of the novice, "mentorable" moments focused on individual students went unexplored.

When interviewed about her work with Nan, Lisette explained that there were times she was careful about timing and not pushing too much at once, and respectful of the needs and receptivity of the teacher. Lisette explains her tailored support:

> My approach depended on if [Nan] was open at that time. She will tell you what her needs are. "Let's save that for next time," she would say. She will always bring up that conversation again. She will say I'm ready to talk about it now. It's more about timing. I'm conscious of not wanting to overwhelm her. Is she really ready to absorb this?

Lisette made moves during conferences that point to a mentor's challenge of reading a novice's "readiness" and deciding when to focus on individual learners and when to structure an entire lesson; when to give solutions to easily solved problems, and when to push reflective thinking to extend the novice's conceptions of learners and strategies to meet their needs. Regardless of reasons, despite use of a scripted observation as assessment tool, a meaningful focus on individual learners and their needs was not sustained.

Analyzing Student Work

As LNTI respondents noted and the cases support, collaborative analysis of student work provides an opportunity to use assessment to guide new teacher growth toward student learning goals. Meg, the mentor in case one, explained, "We so often hear that phrase of let your assessment inform your instruction and no one has ever really said what that looks like. When we do this analysis of student work it is made very clear." Yet, in practice, analysis of student work is a multilayered endeavor that requires much support. The mentor takes the novice through a process of looking at each student's work to understand his or her strengths and challenges in relation to a standard of practice. This first stage is an opportunity to assess learning of specific skills and to know where students are in terms of meeting standards.

Nan and Lisette analyze student work. Lisette guided Nan:

M: This is Andrea . . . where do you think she falls with content of her piece?

T: I feel that she's below, and reaching towards approaching the standard.

M: Do you see any areas that she really excels in besides the editing pieces?

T: I feel like she has voice down.

M: So this is a person that can really elaborate on what she's feeling, what she's thinking, but now we really need to focus in on helping her with the revision. . . . What would be the first things you might pick out to work on with her?

T: Sentence structure.

They worked through the rubric, assessing whether each student addressed each part. Lisette then asked, "How might you support each of these students to move forward?" This scene of dissecting student work highlights the complexity of the endeavor as the mentor guided a teacher to:

1. Identify standards.
2. Assess student performance using a rubric and group student work in categories related to standards.
3. Assess writing strengths and weaknesses.
4. Identify how she will support each student to learn.

Analysis of student work, then, supports understanding student learning needs and differentiating instruction to address them.

Joshua and Meg analyze student work. The following excerpt from Joshua's and Meg's case illustrates this process well. Joshua and Meg were discussing student samples of descriptive writing. It illustrates how Meg probed to help Joshua understand ways to differentiate instruction.

M: We were able to look at what the performance of each [student] was, and what we might do to move the kids forward. What would be the next steps in your planning? How does our assessment guide the instruction that comes next?

T: We talked about taking a student sample that has been exceeding and have them identify components of it that make it exceeding description. . . .

M: OK, so identify qualities that make it exceeding. What might be something else?

T: Give them another opportunity to write descriptively upon doing that, then also applying it to other things like the life-lab.

M: So once they identify the qualities, would you be giving them some of their work back and asking them where they think they are?

T: Yeah, we could do self-assessment. Have them look at their progression since the analysis that they've done on identifying descriptive components. That would be good for them, they can see their own growth. . . .

M: Now is there anything you might do differently with your groups . . . as far as the content or the approach? Let's say if you want them all to be looking at descriptive language, might you be teaching it differently to each group?

T: Yeah. . . . I would have to vary the instruction based on what they need . . .

M: . . . If we know that you might be talking to them about how they're writing about their literature and responding, this gives us a sense of who's where. This kind of analysis of student work, this could also give you a sense of how to approach the groups, and at some point in time it could give you a sense of how to group [or make shifts to regroup].

Meg has taken Joshua through a process of connecting student assessment with next-step planning that focuses on individual learners' needs. The discussion traversed many topics of assessment and instructional scaffolding. The next steps involved further levels of assessment, including student-generated criteria for effective writing, student-self assessment, assessing and planning for different level groups of students, and, ultimately, using assessments to regroup students in more effective learning settings. While Joshua articulated the need for differentiated instruction, his mentor identified a concern about his grouping practices: "The challenge is he hasn't thought a lot about assessing them and moving them around or changing groups." At the end of the excerpt she planted seeds to address this.

Both teachers and both mentors reported novice teacher growth in focusing on individual students' learning that resulted from the mentoring process. Lisette reported:

Analysis of student work was really effective for [Nan]. From the analysis, she realized the writing needs of her students. She developed her writing program based on this and realized she needed to do more small groups and individualized instruction. She is really learning to

differentiate instruction . . . [Nan] as a first year teacher is further
along than most second year teachers.

Nan reported at the end of the year, "My greatest area of improvement was
in working with my English language development students."

Meg and Joshua continued to work together in Joshua's second year of
teaching. At an end-of-the-year interview, Meg identified tremendous growth
in Joshua's teaching and focus on diverse learners, noting he was becoming
an instructional role model for his peers: "His philosophy is 'What approaches
can I do to best meet my students' needs? What's the most effective way to
teach students and meet their diverse needs?'" Joshua reported that his greatest area of growth was in differentiating instruction in literacy, supported
by sorting and assessing student work with his mentor, adding, "I plan to
continue to work more on differentiating instruction in reading and writing
for ELLs." While Meg and Joshua acknowledged growth, there were areas
for further development. Meg reported, "The challenge remains that . . . students in groups didn't often change. He is not yet in the habit of assessing on
a regular basis."

Cases Summary

These mentors revealed knowledge of assessment through a focused
collaborative analysis of classroom data. With mentors, novices at times
developed frames for next-steps instruction for the class and adapted and
tailored work for individual learners, particularly those identified as low
performers. Beginning teachers began to understand how assessment could
inform instruction to meet diverse learners' needs.

The cases also highlight intricacies and challenges of enacting multiple
domains of assessment in the context of classrooms. The mentors needed a
deep knowledge base from which to draw and an excellent ability to "read"
what was needed in the moment and specific context. The cases revealed how
mentors and novices traversed among student self-assessment practices, assessment of individual student learning, assessment of novices' focus on learners, and assessment of novices' needs. The multidimensional processes of
assessment at the level of student, teacher, and mentor created a complex
task for mentor and novice alike. Mentors also were challenged to respond to
pressing concerns of novices while staying focused on individual student learners. Mentors further had to decide when to offer solutions and when to promote novice reflection. Thus, while enacting such a knowledge base prompted
the novice's focus on student learning and low performers, this work occurred
with varying degrees of depth and complexity, due to a mentor's preparedness, disposition, and decisions in the moment.

PROMISES AND CHALLENGES IN USING ASSESSMENT KNOWLEDGE FOR MENTORING

Our study suggests that mentors need multilayered and complex knowledge and abilities related to assessment of students, alignment of curriculum with standards, and formative assessment of the new teacher. This is a tall order that raises issues. First, our participants identified the need for time for mentors to digest grade-level content standards. Given the lack of subject matter and often grade-level fit between mentors and new teachers (e.g., Porter, Youngs, & Odden, 2001), mentors may need significant preparation to know what particular content and grade level standards look like in practice.

Second, our participants noted that mentors need strong knowledge of assessment of students. Yet, novices and veterans alike have reported lack of university preparation and professional development work in innovative classroom assessment practices (Stiggins, 1995). Limited attention to such an essential component of teaching and mentoring suggests that induction programs may need to pay particular attention to developing the mentor's assessment knowledge and skills. This likely would include generalized assessment knowledge (guiding principles, strategies, and tools), and practices for student assessment tied strongly to subject matter and grade level.

Cases we analyzed confirmed the centrality of assessment in the mentor's repertoire of practice in focusing the new teacher on student learners. Our analyses showed some mentors equipped with knowledge in multiple domains of assessment and able to use it to focus new teachers on learners. Mentors asked questions and used follow-up probes. They demonstrated the complexity of using observational data and working closely with new teachers to assess individual students' work, in order to plan relevant, tailored next-steps instruction.

Beyond knowledge and skills, however, dispositions of teachers (and, by extension, mentors) play an important role in how a professional enacts a knowledge base (Feiman-Nemser & Remillard, 1996). Mentors in examples we chose read the mentoring moments to gauge how inquiring to be and how guiding and intervening to be with their mentees. At times, a focus on how the new teacher felt about instruction overrode discussion of strategies that might better meet student needs. This may be attributable to mentors' skill of balancing competing demands and attending to the new teacher's pressing concerns. It also may be due to lack of a clear conception in the field of how a mentor can tutor a new teacher in attending to individual student learning, and how a persistent stance in that area may be necessary.

The cases also highlight the complexity of using knowledge in mentoring conversations that occur in the busy world of schools. Mentors may need to explore collaboratively their mentoring moves and knowledge base in action. Induction leaders and mentors we studied had developed their knowledge in social learning contexts—the mentor/novice pairs in a structured, ongoing, inquiry-rich induction program; the mentors in weekly collaborative mentor professional development; and LNTI members in ongoing action inquiry and network-supported collaborative reflection. To make induction work well, such challenging and knowledge-producing contexts, supported by conceptions of ways to meet student learning needs, likely are needed.

More than ever, mentoring must involve close attention to guiding new teachers to attend to the learning needs of their diverse students. Our study provides some evidence that mentoring new teachers to attend to the learning of their students in their individuality and their diversity can take hold. More longitudinal work is needed to understand ways mentoring can help such learning become central to a novice's concerns. Our study provides clearer evidence, however, that such mentoring is grounded in knowledge of assessment, and that skillful use of that knowledge can bring individual student learning into focus and provide novices with methods for shaping instruction to meet students' varied learning needs.

CONCLUSION

We began by highlighting developmental models of teaching that describe how novices tend to begin careers focused on materials and lessons of instruction, management issues, and performance of self as teacher. Attention to individual student learning typically has followed, often several years later. However, it is possible to interrupt predictable development and focus the novice's attention on individual student learning. This chapter revealed how assessment knowledge and practice can support mentors in doing this important work.

NOTES

1. Among these are the Interstate New Teacher Assessment and Support Consortium Model Standards for Beginning Teacher Licensing and Development, and the California Standards for the Teaching Profession.
2. All names are pseudonyms to maintain confidentiality.

REFERENCES

Athanases, S. Z., & Achinstein, B. (2003). Focusing new teachers on individual and low performing students: The centrality of formative assessment in the mentor's repertoire of practice. *Teachers College Record, 105*(8), 1486–1520.

Bullough, R. V. (1997). Becoming a teacher: Self and the social location of teacher education. In B. J. Biddle, T. L. Good, & I. F. Goodson (Eds.), *The international handbook of teachers and teaching* (pp. 79–134). Dordrecht, Netherlands: Kluwer.

Darling-Hammond, L., Gendler, T., & Wise, A. E. (1990). *The teaching internship.* Santa Monica, CA: Rand Corporation.

Feiman-Nemser, S. (2001). Helping novices learn to teach: Lessons from an exemplary support teacher. *Journal of Teacher Education, 52(1),* 17–30.

Feiman-Nemser, S., & Remillard, J. (1996). Perspectives on learning to teach. In F. B. Murray (Ed.), *The teacher educator's handbook: Building a knowledge base for the preparation of teachers* (pp. 63–91). San Francisco: Jossey-Bass.

Grossman, P. (1990). *The making of a teacher: Teacher knowledge and teacher education.* New York: Teachers College Press.

Grossman, P. L. (1992). Why models matter: An alternate view on professional growth in teaching. *Review of Educational Research, 62(2),* 171–179.

Huling-Austin, L. (Ed.). (1989). *Assisting the beginning teacher.* Reston, VA: Association of Teacher Educators.

Kilbourn, B., & Roberts, G. (1991). May's first year: Conversations with a mentor. *Teachers College Record, 93(2),* 252–264.

Orland, L. (2001). Reading a mentoring situation: One aspect of learning to mentor. *Teaching and Teacher Education, 17(1),* 75–88.

Porter, A., Youngs, P., & Odden, A. (2001). Advances in teacher assessments and their uses. In V. Richardson (Ed.), *Handbook of research on teaching* (4th ed., pp. 259–297). Washington, DC: American Educational Research Association.

Richardson, V., & Placier, P. (2001). Teacher change. In V. Richardson (Ed.), *Handbook of research on teaching* (4th ed., pp. 905–947). Washington, DC: American Educational Research Association.

Shulman, L. S. (1987). Knowledge and teaching: Foundations of the new reform. *Harvard Educational Review, 57(1),* 1–22.

Stiggins, R. (1995, November). Assessment literacy for the 21st century. *Phi Delta Kappan,* 238–245.

Wang, J. (2001). Contexts of mentoring and opportunities for learning to teach: A comparative study of mentoring practice. *Teaching and Teacher Education, 17(1),* 51–73.

CHAPTER 2

Mentors' Knowledge of Equity and Diversity: Maintaining a Bifocal Perspective on New Teachers and Their Students

*Betty Achinstein and
Steven Z. Athanases*

How can mentors support new teachers to meet the needs of diverse learners? New teachers in the United States, especially those underprepared, are disproportionately placed in classrooms with students of color, from low-income families, and with limited English proficiency (Darling-Hammond, 1997; Lankford, Loeb, & Wyckoff, 2002; Oakes, 1990; Shields et al., 2001). Even with basic preparation, most novices need ongoing support to meet all students' needs, and for those on emergency credentials, support is even more critical, or many students in their classes likely will be underserved. Mentoring holds promise in providing needed support. However, we know little about the expertise needed to mentor novices on equity and diversity, and what it looks like in action.

To contribute to this important area of inquiry, we examined how experienced mentors and induction leaders characterize what mentors need to know and be able to do to focus new teachers on diversity and equity, and what this knowledge base looks like in practice from an in-depth case study of a mentor and her new teacher. We explore the problematic nature of this

---

Mentors in the Making: Developing New Leaders for New Teachers, edited by Betty Achinstein and Steven Z. Athanases. Copyright © 2006 by Teachers College, Columbia University. All rights reserved. Prior to photocopying items for classroom use, please contact the Copyright Clearance Center, Customer Service, 222 Rosewood Dr., Danvers, MA 01923, USA, tel. (978) 750-8400.

work, then discuss the multidimensional knowledge base of mentoring for equity and its educational implications.

MENTORING FOR EQUITY AND DIVERSITY

Equity concerns persistent patterns of difference in educational opportunities and achievement among students. Broadly speaking, the primary gap in the United States exists between white, native-English-speaking, middle- to high-income students on one hand, and generally lower-income, culturally and linguistically diverse (primarily Latino and African American) students on the other. Equity refers to a state in which the gap is eliminated and the achievement of all is raised; it also refers, at times, to measures needed to close the gap. Access to opportunities for all means providing differentiated supports for learners (Haycock, 2001). Also necessary is challenging current inequitable practices to transform schools into more socially just and equitable systems (Freire, 1983; Sleeter & Grant, 1999). Affirming diversity is to celebrate its richness and to understand how diversity enhances learning for all (e.g., Nieto, 2004). However, this work also requires knowledge of structural inequities that persist in the larger societal contexts in which schools are situated. This includes understanding the ways in which race, ethnicity, language, and class impact teaching, learning, and schooling.

Working toward equity requires developing cultural competence. This includes teachers' knowledge of their own, students', and school cultures; how to teach content to diverse learners; and how to use culture in teaching (Ladson-Billings, 2001). Focusing novice teachers on equity and diversity is a particular challenge. New teachers in the United States are predominantly white, middle-class, and monolingual and often are unprepared to meet the needs of the culturally and linguistically diverse students whom they very likely will teach. They may have negative assumptions about diverse learners due to a cultural mismatch with students (Guskey, 1995). Also, novices often have unelaborated schemata of children from their apprenticeship of observation (Lortie, 1975). Novices have limited instructional repertoires and resources specifically focused on diverse learners.

In our study, we first asked: What do mentors need to know and be able to do to focus new teachers on diversity and equity? We posed this question to 37 veteran mentors and new teacher program directors in the Leadership Network for Teacher Induction (see Introduction) and asked for illustrations from practice. Our second research question asked: What does this knowledge base of mentoring for equity look like in practice, and what are its complexities? To answer this, we looked inside one teacher induction program represented in the network, drawing a case from a set of 20 mentor–mentee pairs in a larger 2-year study. Informed by research on the knowledge base for teaching (Feiman-Nemser & Remillard, 1996; Grossman, 1990; Shulman, 1987), we examined questionnaires and developed new categories that reflected mentors' conceptions. Case data were analyzed for particular patterns identified in questionnaire results and to provide depth and contrast. (For discussion of the full study, see Achinstein and Athanases, 2005.)

MENTOR KNOWLEDGE AND ABILITIES

Analyses of questionnaire responses from 37 induction leaders yielded four domains of knowledge needed to mentor new teachers on issues of diversity and equity, highlighted here.

Pedagogical Knowledge

Participants overwhelmingly identified pedagogical knowledge as the most essential in mentoring for equity. This included knowledge of ways to teach diverse *youth*, and knowledge of ways to teach or guide *teachers* during mentor sessions in ways that promote equitable learning.

Classrooms. Participants identified that mentoring for equity includes knowing strategies to establish a trusting classroom climate, build community, and hold high expectations for all students. It includes scaffolding lessons for all students, multiple modes of lesson presentation, and differentiating instruction to individual needs. Mentors benefit from, according to participants, research on multiple intelligences and learning styles/resiliency, and knowledge that "designing lesson/units for higher levels of engagement will not only increase learning but lower distraction in [the] work environment."

Participants reported how effective mentors know how curriculum supports learning of all students through content integration (Banks, 2003), the infusion of diverse racial, cultural, and linguistic content. Also important is tapping local funds of knowledge (Moll & Vellez-Ibanez, 1992) so that students, families, and cultural and community experiences are included in lessons. Mentors also use standards to guide pedagogy: "If I have some familiarity with grade-level content standards, I can better talk about where any one student is . . . [which is] critical to working on closing the achievement gap." Academic development of ELLs was central to what mentors need to know, including research-informed practice, what one participant called "An understanding of the stages of language development and other second language theories and what students are capable of doing at each stage so that teachers can differentiate instruction." This knowledge includes specific approaches to support language instruction and development of academic literacy, including techniques of SDAIE (Specially Designed Academic Instruction in English).

Pedagogy to focus teachers on diversity and equity in mentoring sessions. Beyond classroom pedagogy, participants noted that effective mentors know how to use a mentoring session as a strategic site to focus novices on diversity and equity. Starting with individual students and their learning was fundamental: "Help new teachers realize they are teaching kids, not algebra, and how important it is to let kids know you care about them as individuals." Beyond this, participants noted that mentors can sharpen attention to equity and diversity by embedding these concerns in weekly conversations, using observational data to help the teacher analyze equitable learning opportunities. One participant noted: "Always look for who is left out and who benefits. Don't be afraid to gently name the dynamics you see." The mentor also can tap local teachers "who are meeting the needs of diverse populations so they can provide opportunities for the novice to see effective practices."

Participants were clear, though, that many new teachers are unprepared or unwilling to address equity in their instruction. This calls for gauging a teacher's knowledge of self related to such concerns. Mentors also need a repertoire of supports, including attending to individuality of teachers and an "ability to listen to teacher reflection and move that into a conversation that assists the teacher to look at a practice in a new way." The mentor can use data to prod a resistant teacher to be more reflective about equity. A participant illustrated:

> The beginning teacher made a judgmental statement about which students would be on task. So [the mentor] did a scripted observation, which included both a focus on a particular student and an every-five-minute tally of on-task behavior. The teacher examined the data and was surprised to see that her "hypothesis" was not supported by the data. [The mentor] began a conversation that will continue for many weeks.

Mentoring for equity includes knowing how to move the resistant teacher past a narrow or racist perspective. As one participant noted, this involves helping the teacher with "an attitude awareness shift without lecturing and/ or pointing out that the new teacher's existing stance and values may be unexamined and limited."

Knowledge of Contexts

Mentors also need to know how pedagogy is situated in nested contexts relevant to the lives of diverse students and teachers. At the local level, mentors have to help teachers learn about local cultures and communities, and know how to help novices negotiate their professional worlds as they work to meet diverse learners' needs. This includes knowing "how to work effectively with the cultures by knowing the history, values, family ties and cultural specifics" of local groups. The effective mentor, according to several participants, knows ways to access this information, including district documents, community agencies, helpful people and material, and even a bus ride through student communities. Knowing local cultural knowledge serves the mentor. One participant recalled mentoring a teacher who panicked during Black History Month because of a lack of materials. Together they created a library and invited students and families to share culture and stories throughout the year, not just during one month.

Local knowledge also includes how to identify "inequities in content, methodology, treatment of students, and system." It includes how to "coach for equity" with a teacher, attending also to "a community of teachers, and a system" (school/district). This last component signals how several participants cast mentors as change agents who understand how classrooms are embedded within inequitable school and district contexts and who can transform them.

Also important, according to participants, is knowing broader social issues such as "the systemic underpinnings of racism in our society" and "white privilege and how to see it." Mentors need a conceptual understanding of terms and need to know how "diversity" has varied features, including race, language, gender, and socioeconomic status. Also vital is knowing how broader social realities shape inequitable educational opportunities. The effective mentor uses this knowledge to work toward closing the achievement gap between groups who traditionally perform well in particular schooling contexts and those who do not.

Knowledge of Learners

Responses identified how mentors can help novices see diverse youth as resources and not merely as "problems." This includes helping new teachers move past a distanced "othering" of students different from themselves, to a closer knowing of individuals. One participant remarked, "It is the personal attention and connection that is remembered." This includes being unafraid to inquire about factors shaping students' classroom learning:

"Why does José not do homework (sleep in class)? Is that because he is working 40 hours per week to help support his family?"

The mentor may need to be on the lookout for new teachers seeing nonmainstream students through deficit lenses. One participant stated: "If students who are acquiring English are all described as 'discipline problems' by the teacher, it is the mentor's job to present these data and work with the teacher on possible solutions." Another recalled how a new teacher focused on some children "cheating" on tests because they were underprepared for them. As a mentor, this participant had to help the teacher see how using a single assessment, a test based almost solely on homework, was privileging some students and producing high failure rates for students who apparently were unable to secure equitable parental assistance with homework at night. The teacher needed guidance to examine practice and to see other ways to support all students as potential learners. One participant stated: "You can't increase student achievement until you believe all students . . . culturally/ linguistically diverse . . . are capable, gifted and talented children."

Mentor's Knowledge of Self

The final domain was mentors' knowledge of self related to diversity and equity and the ability to evolve. According to respondents, mentors need to have engaged in self-reflection on their attitudes toward educational inequities and their own relevant beliefs, values, and practices. This includes confronting one's own positions and prejudices and understanding biases one brings to a mentoring relationship. According to participants, mentors also should be open to their own sense of inadequacy in confronting these issues. Like most educators working in highly diverse classrooms, mentors may not find the work easy. Central, however, is the ability to be comfortable discussing these issues openly and honestly. Mentors must remain open to diverse points of view and commit to making change themselves as they come to understand complexities of mentoring for equity. One participant noted, "Without having done some self-reflection on equity, how can the mentor be expected to coach a new teacher in this area? It's important to keep your own house in order before helping others."

SONYA AND MAGGIE: A CASE STUDY

Examining a case of mentoring for equity exposes nuances and tensions of a knowledge base in action. Sonya[1] was identified by induction program leaders as expert on equity issues, particularly in working with ELLs. A white woman in her 40s, Sonya was a 4th-year mentor who led professional development on equity. She articulated knowledge of herself related to equity: "I feel as a teacher and a mentor if you are not consistently challenging the system, you're furthering it." Maggie, a white woman in her 20s, was a new teacher at a K–5 school with 96% Latino students, 66% low-income, and 55% ELLs. Maggie's grade-level colleagues drew straws to decide who would work with each group. Maggie drew the short straw and therefore received the "low" language-ability-tracked 4th graders. Her more experienced colleagues drew the "highs" and "middles." Sonya remarked on the inequitable nature of this process: "It doesn't make any sense to decide who gets the most challenged reading group by drawing straws and leaving that to the new teacher." Maggie was confronted with a classroom full of ELLs and students with varied skill sets, six identified as "nonreaders."

Both Maggie and Sonya described their mentoring relationship as positive and collaborative. However, one equity-focused problem Sonya addressed with Maggie concerned Maggie's beliefs and practices related to ELLs and her capacity to "differentiate instruction." Sonya found that Maggie shifted instruction downward, not challenging learners, and not recognizing different needs of students. Here Sonya tapped her classroom pedagogical knowledge for equity in articulating high expectations for all students and the importance of differentiation. But it was her additional knowledge of contexts about broader social issues that enabled her to identify these as equity concerns. By situating a problematic labeling of "low learners" in a context of inequitable school practices, Sonya brought a larger equity lens to the classroom interaction. She explained:

> There is a culture among teachers who've accepted that these kids are of limited intelligences . . . designated as "low learners." They are not being treated as ten-year-olds, but as six-year-olds. It's totally humiliating to their intelligence and what they are capable of doing. You would never see that in a white, middle-class school where parents are empowered.

Sonya used mentoring conferences to push Maggie's thinking about creating "dependence" among her ELLs, repeatedly reading aloud to them and rarely extending them to develop their own reading or comprehension abilities to promote academic language. She also wanted to help Maggie differentiate instruction, address different stages of language development of the learners, and not teach to the lowest common denominator.

Sonya's case most importantly demonstrates pedagogical knowledge for focusing the teacher on equity in mentoring sessions. Sonya found her opening when Maggie raised a concern that she didn't know what students could do independently and that she scaffolded so much that she did not know their abilities to work on their own (M = Mentor; T = Teacher).

> *M:* How does differentiation look given that it's a whole-group activity and it sounds like quite a diverse group since you've got the six who are not comprehending independently yet?
> *T:* The only differentiation would be, for the lower kids, reading it out loud, they're following along . . .
> *M:* . . . You started out with, "How do I know what they can do on their own" and along with it "How do I give them the maximum opportunity to do what they can do on their own." I'm wondering if you're not depriving the other 17 students of a chance to see what they can get on their own before you read it to them.

Sonya explained varied ways to teach to different learners, with more intensive vocabulary work for some while pushing for independent comprehension from others. She provided strategies, careful not to sound too directive:

> I don't want to take over. You might want to keep it simpler, but . . . not letting the differentiation for the very beginners keep the others from trying to get it on their own first. . . . Some of the kids who wind up in these so-called "low-intensive groups," one of their issues is they become more teacher-dependent.

The mentor was respectful to keep pace with the novice (starting with Maggie's concern), was not too directive, yet helped her consider more equitable practices. Sonya highlighted knowledge of *student learners:* differentiating the 6 from the 17, assessing the novice's challenges, and confronting Maggie about students growing dependent. Sonya also appreciated the novice's needs as an *adult learner,* making suggestions but not "taking over":

> I was constantly scanning and searching for an opportunity in the discussion. I kept coming back to that these people are capable of reading for themselves. They have some ability to look at print and make sense. Every one of them, even if they are low. I have to find an opening for her to find that.

When Sonya asked Maggie how she felt the lesson went, Maggie said she thought it went well. Sonya later remarked that her biggest challenge was:

> to find a way to honor what she had done and to find some kind of way in to see if she was still going to be open for a next step to allow

students to answer questions on their own. To do something to allow them to demonstrate their comprehension or lack of it.

Sonya used observational data that described what students were doing and saying to challenge Maggie's thinking. Sonya also interjected pushing questions and prompts: "I can't tell for sure where the students got this information from, you reading it or reading it themselves," and "Is there an opportunity for students to recheck their predictions?" Sonya reported to Maggie that there was almost "no higher-level thinking in all of the lesson," and that assessing predictions would contribute some higher-level thinking.

By the end of the observation cycle and conferences with her mentor, Maggie was beginning to rethink some of her ideas about students and her practice: "I know next time I would do things differently. . . . A real aha I had from the observation and feedback process is about giving them a chance to do more on their own so that I can get to know their independent comprehension level." Maggie identified that over the year she had learned more about differentiating instruction, meeting the needs of all learners, learning to pull out a small group for extra support, and using multiple strategies to scaffold. However, she saw this as an area for continued growth.

In focusing Maggie on equity, Sonya highlighted tensions between the mentor's knowledge of adult learners' sensitivities and knowledge of broader social inequities for student learners. Sonya chose not to confront Maggie with a critique of school inequities:

My goal in the political sense is not something I can hit head-on with her. It's not going to make sense to her about how there is a whole cultural social thing that allows a whole group of teachers to look down on kids and expect less of them without even realizing they are doing it. That's not someplace I would go with her. But I want her to see who the students are as human beings and what they are capable of.

Sonya also showed care in her critique of Maggie: "Some teachers, if you tell them what you think, they feel criticized and then shut down. Maggie is like that. So it's kind of a cross between giving her information that she is really lacking, but not doing it in any blaming way."

Using knowledge of professional contexts, Sonya noted her challenge:

The principal thinks everything Maggie is doing is great and the other teachers want her to make her class as rote as possible . . . So, I'm working pretty much against everyone around her. I think I'm the only one who would bring that point of view in . . . and she was a little bit resistant to hearing it.

Sonya reported that the equity work would challenge Maggie's relationships at her school: "She is going to have to think critically about her peers and the principal when she does that."

At times Sonya saw her role as reaching out to several educators over the 4 years she worked with novices there. She spoke of challenges and of hope: "I have to try and impact higher-level things that I know are not good for kids. It's an activist role if you get them to question academic tracking, and work with a number of teachers and the principal to encourage them to question the system." Sonya's nonconfrontational stance is one among several that a mentor might take. Nonetheless, the case reveals challenges of this work and how one mentor taps a knowledge base for equity-focused mentoring and uses it judiciously to enact change with a novice teacher.

MENTORS' EQUITY KNOWLEDGE BASE AND CHALLENGES

Knowledge reported by induction leaders in our study maps onto previous research on teachers' knowledge in three broad domains: (1) curriculum and teaching; (2) contexts and purposes; and (3) learners and learning (Darling-Hammond, Wise, & Klein, 1999). It also reinforces research on equity-focused teacher education with themes including new teacher inquiry into inequitable practices, culturally relevant pedagogy, and teaching that fosters language development and language self-esteem (e.g., Cochran-Smith, 1995; Garcia, 1996; Ladson-Billings, 2001; Zeichner et al., 1998). However, our study makes important contributions in three areas of knowledge needed in mentoring for equity, described below.

A Bilevel Knowledge Base and Bifocal Perspective

Each knowledge domain in mentoring for equity has a bilevel nature, highlighted in Figure 2.1 drawn from our analyses. Across domains, the bottom row of the figure marks how targeting students undergirds mentoring for equity. However, the upper row (targeting teachers) shows how effective mentors also use nuanced approaches to address needs of the adult learner in context. To enact a bilevel knowledge base, the mentor assumes a *bifocal perspective* on teachers and students. Up close the mentor focuses on the novice, what she or he knows and needs. The mentor simultaneously holds the big picture in view, which is the students, their learning, and their needs.

For the domain of pedagogy, effective mentors target students through knowledge of strategies to teach diverse youth and promote equity. However, for work with teachers, mentors need strategies for observation, feedback, and critique that focus the novice on classroom inequities. For knowledge

Figure 2.1. A Bilevel Knowledge Base for Equity-Focused Mentoring of New Teachers

Knowledge Domain

	Pedagogy	Contexts	Learners	Self
Targeting Teachers	Wide repertoire of mentoring strategies and stances for observation, assessment, feedback, and critique in mentoring conversations that guide teaching reform; commitments and practices to focus the novice on challenges of inequity in the classroom	Embedded professional contexts; broader social contexts of schooling and teaching; leadership and change agency	Assessment of novice assets and needs about issues of equity; new teacher as adult learner; novice knowledge base, strategies, and cultural competence; novice's reflectivity level and receptivity to change	Focusing the novice on own identity vis-à-vis student diversity
Targeting Students	Wide repertoire of strategies to serve all learners; repertoire of strategies to serve culturally and linguistically diverse youth and to promote equity	Local school culture: student, parent, community; broader social and structural issues of inequity and discrimination	Assessment of students' funds of knowledge and challenges to deficit views; learning theory and culturally responsive learning theory	Mentors' understanding of self related to student diversity and equity; awareness of own biases, stances, and interactions with students

48

of contexts that targets students, the mentor uses awareness of local and larger issues related to inequities. The upper row, however, marks how effective mentoring for equity always is embedded within a new teacher's complex professional world that the mentor must help the new teacher negotiate and, at times, transform.

In knowledge of learners, the bottom row shows how mentors need to know ways new teachers can learn about their diverse students. Also, the upper row shows how effective mentors know their new teachers well to guide them in pedagogy that affirms equity for students. While a mentor builds rapport and understands an individual teacher's needs and readiness, the mentor also holds out larger goals and tries to lead the novice on a pathway. Sonya listened to Maggie's concerns about student independence, built on these ideas, and probed for changes in differentiation, expectations, and practices with ELLs. Finally, Figure 2.1 shows the last column of knowledge of self. Effective mentors reflect on their own understandings and biases regarding diversity and equity and, in work with novices, promote similar reflection.

Pedagogical Learner Knowledge

Respondents' most reported domain in mentoring for equity was pedagogical knowledge for teaching students and for guiding teachers. In the most influential models of the knowledge base for teaching (e.g., Grossman, 1990; Shulman, 1987), this domain aligns best with general pedagogical knowledge. In our earlier analyses and as demonstrated by Sonya's practices in the case, we were struck by how the pedagogical knowledge seldom was "general." Just as "pedagogical content knowledge" captures an amalgam of subject matter knowledge and pedagogical knowledge, we found the pedagogy that our case and respondents described (for classroom teaching and new teacher mentoring) was deeply informed by knowledge of diverse learners and knowledge of contexts. In this sense, they evidenced *pedagogical learner knowledge* (Grimmett & MacKinnon, 1992). This includes "knowledge that allows teachers to understand learners from different cultural, social, and family backgrounds, interpret properly what they say and do, and support effectively their development in cognitive, social, physical, and psychological dimensions" (Wang & Odell, 2002, p. 486). As an amalgam of general pedagogical knowledge and knowledge of learners and contexts, pedagogical learner knowledge is "pedagogical procedural information useful in enhancing learner-focused teaching in the dailyness of classroom action," or the ways teachers interact "rigorously and supportively with learners" (Grimmett & MacKinnon, 1992, p. 387).

The knowledge base for teaching generally includes attention to differentiating instruction. Shulman (1987) noted how a thoughtful teacher *adapts* a lesson to different classes of students, and, within classes, *tailors* instruction to varied students' needs. In the Teacher Assessment Project at Stanford, high scoring teachers demonstrated greater ability to reflect on how instruction relates to individuals and groups of learners and to reconstruct a learning situation for different student groups as needed (Athanases, 1993). However, pedagogical learner knowledge assumes there is a body of knowledge, skills, and dispositions particular to working with culturally and linguistically diverse youth in the 21st century, and that knowing such things shapes teaching and mentoring for equity and diversity.

Our analyses advance a theoretical understanding of a knowledge base for effective mentoring related to diverse learners and promoting equity. New teachers often begin ill-prepared to understand cultural and linguistic backgrounds of their students, and with limited repertoires of pedagogy and curriculum. Effective mentors are equipped to guide, question, and challenge these novices as they begin their careers. However, mentoring in such contexts requires more than general pedagogical knowledge. It requires an instructional repertoire informed by an understanding of larger social contexts that have shaped educational inequities, cultural norms for learning, and language development, and how they play out in class. A mentor needs to know what it means to break down complex texts, to make texts accessible in a learnable language for ELLs. Effective mentors use a vast repertoire of differentiating and scaffolding strategies specific to distinct developmental phases of ELLs, including equitable participation structures to develop language and self-esteem, assessing understandings in writing and speech, language development, comprehension, and challenges to language acquisition. Mentors need to understand the needs and strengths of novices as learners, receptivity to change and consciousness of equity concerns, and contexts in which the novice works. All of this knowledge deeply informs pedagogical insights and stances mentors hold, a very particular kind of pedagogical learner knowledge to focus novices on equity and diversity.

Challenges of Enacting the Knowledge Base

Mentoring for equity involves challenges. First, an effective mentor must be equipped to move new teachers beyond a focus on their own performance to that of individual learners, and to ways to differentiate instruction for highly diverse students. Second, mentors confront resistance and "dysconscious" assumptions (King, 1991) about linguistically and culturally diverse students. Mentoring, like teaching, for equity involves moral dimensions (Hargreaves, 1995; Kelchtermans & Hamilton, 2004) of persisting in focusing on all students' learning, while addressing adult learners' needs. Third, equity-focused mentors face the political challenge of critiquing failure in schooling. Should mentoring transmit knowledge about current arrangements or use knowledge transformation, where mentors help novices "learn to teach against the grain" (Cochran-Smith, 1991; Cochran-Smith & Paris, 1995)? While Sonya worked to change inequitable assumptions and practices of a single novice teacher, she was continually challenged to counter the larger school culture and structures that may have been reproducing inequalities through tracking and lowered expectations. Further, focusing on equity for students puts the mentor in a bind. Sonya had to consider that in trying to create more equitable conditions for students, she may be putting Maggie at risk by placing her at odds with the political context of the school's adult community.

CONCLUSION

We have described a complex mentor knowledge base for focusing novice teachers on equity, with lessons for practice, research, and policy in induction and mentor development. Current approaches to induction policy and funding, mentor recruitment, and professional development may lack the supports necessary for development of such a complex knowledge base. Programs that recruit expert teachers and do not support mentor development in pedagogical learner knowledge for students and adults will leave mentors ill-equipped to focus novices on diverse learners' needs. Mentor leaders in our study engaged in ongoing professional development and collaborative inquiry that included an equity focus, with expert outsiders, readings, resources, and examination and critique of practice. If we want to develop a knowledge base that many mentors never learned in their own preservice or in-service development, then mentors may benefit from new knowledge, access to theory, case studies (like Sonya's), and practice. Also critical are opportunities to learn from other mentors through dialogue, observations, and analysis of videos of practice, as well as opportunities to reflect on their own assumptions about equity and the struggles of focusing novices on equity. Such work requires a community of practice for mentors, with equity and diversity deeply embedded in the work, not arising merely as add-ons.

Research on a knowledge base for mentoring for equity can be further developed through investigations in a range of contexts that feature varied (and intersecting) equity issues including race and ethnicity, socioeconomics, language, gender, and sexual orientation. This research must examine the often unexplored terrain of actual mentor–mentee exchanges over time, capturing dialogue, and exploring impact on beliefs and classroom practices.

Finally, this study provides lessons for school and district policies. The work of educational equity goes beyond that of the mentor, involving administrator leadership and school restructuring to eliminate the kinds of tracking and lowered expectations evident in Maggie's school. Districts also may want to examine mentor recruitment to reflect diverse student populations. Further, mentors must be given time and opportunity to develop cultural understandings of students and teachers with whom they work. Finally, schools and districts must provide time and resources for mentors and novices to meet continuously to conduct this complex work. If mentors hold a key to closing the achievement gap, then researchers, policymakers, and practitioners must turn their attention to articulating the knowledge base and supports necessary to foster the novice's focus on equity.

NOTE

1. All names are pseudonyms to maintain confidentiality.

REFERENCES

Achinstein, B., & Athanases, S. (2005). Focusing new teachers on diversity and equity: Toward a knowledge base for mentors. *Teaching and Teacher Education, 21*(4).

Athanases, S. Z. (1993). Adapting and tailoring lessons: Fostering teacher reflection to meet varied student needs. *Teacher Education Quarterly, 20*(1), 71–81.

Banks, J. A. (2003). Multicultural education: Characteristics and goals. In J. A. Banks & C. A. McGee Banks (Eds.), *Multicultural education: Issues and perspectives* (4th ed., pp. 3–30). New York: Wiley.

Cochran-Smith, M. (1991). Learning to teach against the grain. *Harvard Educational Review, 61*(3), 279–310.

Cochran-Smith, M. (1995). Color blindness and basket making are not the answers: Confronting the dilemmas of race, culture, and language diversity in teacher education. *American Educational Research Journal, 33*(3), 493–522.

Cochran-Smith, M., & Paris, P. (1995). Mentor and mentoring: Did Homer have it right? In J. Smith (Ed.), *Critical discourses on teacher development* (pp. 181–202). London: Cassell.

Darling-Hammond, L. (1997). *Doing what matters most: Investing in quality teaching.* New York: National Commission on Teaching and America's Future.

Darling-Hammond, L., Wise, A. E., & Klein, S. P. (1999). *A license to teach: Raising standards for teaching.* San Francisco: Jossey-Bass.

Feiman-Nemser, S., & Remillard, J. (1996). Perspectives on learning to teach. In F. B. Murray (Ed.), *The teacher educator's handbook: Building a knowledge base for the preparation of teachers* (pp. 63–91). San Francisco: Jossey-Bass.

Friere, P. (1983). *Pedagogy of the oppressed* (M. B. Ramos, Trans.). New York: Continuum.

Garcia, E. E. (1996). Preparing instructional professionals for linguistically and culturally diverse students. In J. Sikula, T. J. Buttery, & E. Guyton (Eds.), *Handbook of research on teacher education* (2nd ed., pp. 802–813). New York: Simon & Schuster Macmillan.

Grimmett, P., & Mackinnon, A. (1992). Craft knowledge and the education of teachers. In G. Grant (Ed.), *Review of research in education* (pp. 385–456). Washington, DC: American Educational Research Association.

Grossman, P. (1990). *The making of a teacher: Teacher knowledge and teacher education*. New York: Teachers College Press.

Guskey, T. R. (1995). Professional development in education: In search of the optimal mix. In T. Guskey & M. Huberman (Eds.), *Professional development in education: New paradigms and practices* (pp. 114–132). New York: Teachers College Press.

Hargreaves, A. (1995). Development and desire: A postmodern perspective. In T. R. Guskey & M. Huberman (Eds.), *Professional development in education: New paradigms and practices* (pp. 9–34). New York: Teachers College Press.

Haycock, K. (2001). Closing the achievement gap. *Educational Leadership, 58*(6), 6–11.

Kelchtermans, G., & Hamilton, M. L. (2004). The dialectics of passion and theory: Exploring the relation between self-study and emotion. In J. Loughran, M. L. Hamilton, V. LaBoskey, & T. Russell (Eds.), *International handbook of research of self-study of teaching and teacher education practices* (pp. 785–810). Dordrecht, Netherlands: Kluwer Publishers.

King, J. (1991). Dysconscious racism: Ideology, identity, and the miseducation of teachers. *Journal of Negro Education, 60*(2), 133–146.

Ladson-Billings, G. (2001). *Crossing over to Canaan: The journey of new teachers in diverse classrooms*. San Francisco: Jossey-Bass.

Lankford, H., Loeb, S., & Wyckoff, J. (2002). Teacher sorting and the plight of urban schools: A descriptive analysis. *Educational Evaluation and Policy Analysis, 24*(1), 37–62.

Lortie, D. (1975). *School teacher: A sociological study*. Chicago: University of Chicago Press.

Moll, L., & Vellez-Ibanez, C. (1992). Funds of knowledge for teaching: Using a qualitative approach to connect homes and classrooms. *Theory into Practice, 31*, 132–141.

Nieto, S. (2004). *Affirming diversity* (4th ed.). New York: Allyn and Bacon.

Oakes, J. (1990). *Multiplying inequities: The effects of race, social class, and tracking on opportunities to learn mathematics and science*. Santa Monica, CA: Rand Corporation.

Shields, P. M., Humphrey, D. C., Wechsler, M. E., Riehl, L. M., Tiffany-Morales, J., Woodworth, K., Young, V. M., & Price, T. (2001). *Teaching and California's future: The status of the teaching profession 2001*. Santa Cruz, CA: The Center for the Future of Teaching and Learning.

Shulman, L. S. (1987). Knowledge and teaching: Foundations of the new reform. *Harvard Educational Review, 57*(1), 1–22.

Sleeter, C. E., & Grant, C. A. (1999). *Making choices for multicultural education: Five approaches to race, class, and gender.* Upper Saddle River, NJ: Prentice-Hall.

Wang, J., & Odell, S. J. (2002). Mentored learning to teach according to standards-based reform: A critical review. *Review of Educational Research, 72*(3), 481–546.

Zeichner, K. M., Grant, C., Gay, G., Gillett, M., Valli, L., & Villegas, A. M. (1998). A research-informed vision of good practice in multicultural teacher education: Design principles. *Theory into Practice, 37*(2), 163–171.

CHAPTER 3

Making Equity Explicit: A Professional Development Model for New Teacher Mentors

Enid Lee

For 2 years I worked intensively with new teacher mentors in California induction programs to explore applying an antiracist, equity-centered lens to the practice of mentoring. Having engaged in antiracist professional development of educators for two decades across Canada and the United States, I felt this new context had promising features: ongoing collaborative work, reflection on needs of adult learners, institutional support, and demographic variety. In addition, some of the mentor programs were represented in the Leadership Network for Teacher Induction (LNTI), where I provided some professional development. This chapter reflects significant steps in my own journey with these mentors. I begin by reporting themes that emerged from 68 mentors' self-assessment of ways they address issues of language, culture, and race in mentoring. I highlight strengths and challenges identified in their practices. Second, I describe key elements of the professional development series I designed and implemented to address the salient issues. I point to promising practices that resulted from this work. Finally, I recommend ways to address dilemmas inherent in moving mentors and new teachers toward racial equality in teacher induction and student achievement.

MENTORS REFLECT ON THEIR EQUITY
STRENGTHS AND CHALLENGES

To prepare, I asked these mentors to reflect on how they address language, race, and culture in mentoring. I coded their reflections as stepping-stones (strengths) and stumbling blocks (challenges). The themes highlight complexities of a knowledge base needed to mentor for equity and shaped the professional development I designed for them.

Stepping-Stones

Four themes of strength emerged. First, respondents reported mentoring novices on English language learner (ELL) needs. Specifically, they highlighted demonstrating lessons for new teachers that enhanced English language development (ELD) and promoted sheltered English strategies. Respondents also described how they marshaled resources by directing new teachers to antiracist, antihomophobic, and linguistically appropriate resources and professional development to deepen novices' knowledge of diverse learners.

Second, mentors explained how they assisted beginning teachers in building lessons by drawing on students' background to stimulate new knowledge and help them gain access to the curriculum. They encouraged novices to recognize differences among students and to provide opportunities for students to learn from each other by sharing their unique experiences. Further, they helped teachers create a welcoming climate for new students to the classroom, moving toward a goal of what one mentor described as "social inclusion."

Third, respondents reported self- and group assessments of awareness levels on issues of equity. For example, one mentor wrote, "[Equity] is a huge issue. . . . We have much to learn . . . and so far to go." According to another, "We're all on a continuum as far as our awareness and sensitivity to these issues." Finally, some mentors expressed general openness to enhancing their awareness. It should be noted though that there was a notable range of awareness levels in the group. The following statements reflect points along a continuum on which they saw themselves: from a complete sense of confidence to clear acknowledgment of difficulty. One mentor wrote in response to the prompt, "How do you address issues of language, culture, and race in your role as mentor?": "Very openly! It's of utmost importance." In contrast, another responded, "This is one of the more difficult questions I have been asked." Still another replied, "I am not uncomfortable with the topics, but because I'm white and middle-class, I know I have blind spots."

Stumbling Blocks

Mentors' responses also point to three challenges that helped focus my subsequent design of professional development for these mentors. First, mentors were much more confident with questions of language and culture than with race. The invisibility of race and its role in education was identified as a major stumbling block. For example, one mentor explained that in approaching teachers, she did not consider issues of language, race, and culture first. She noted: "What I respond to is why they have requested assistance. I look at them as 'fellow teachers.' I look at them as educators and not as members of a particular race. I abhor tribalism." This mentor's remarks demonstrated a collegial response but did not include consideration of how educators' experiences are racialized, or how laws and customs in the United States grant or deny opportunity based on race. Another mentor expressed a disconnect between instruction, student performance, and issues of race, language, and culture. "I haven't met with a new teacher with [his or her] race or culture or language in mind. I have met with the goal of improving delivery of instruction."

Questions of race appeared to remain invisible unless the student populations were identified as "diverse" and thus the issues deemed "relevant." Several mentors responded to issues "if they come up" or if they were "obvious." One mentor explained, "I discuss these matters with my new teachers because both the schools where I work are richly diverse schools." Central to this invisibility was the absence of recognition that racism is systemic and institutional. Some mentors tended to see racism as an episode rather than as a feature of an unequal system that does not serve everyone equally well. Mentors identified the need to make sure that "the new teachers' classrooms should be inclusive," but sometimes missed how in their role as mentors they would have to support new teachers in disrupting inequitable practices, and in specifically identifying what was excluded in order to make the new teachers' classroom inclusive.

The focus on specific social group membership was the second stumbling block for mentors, since the undifferentiated term "all students" seemed to be the preferred way of thinking. The desire "not to attach labels," in part, prevented this examination of group experience. As one respondent explained, "I think the terms I use in discussion with teachers include the language of 'meeting the needs of all students.' . . . I am not thinking of issues of race and gender. Just *all* students." Yet, in order to get at the "all," I have found that educators must specifically identify the groups that make up the "all."

The third stumbling block was that this set of challenges was further exacerbated by the culture of coaching that emphasized relationship building. The coaching model quite correctly supports building trusting relationships between mentor and new teacher. However, because race and racism are often difficult questions to raise, they might be set aside, at least for a while, in order to avoid damaging the relationship. A mentor described a challenging mentoring moment with a new teacher who had her students read aloud an excerpt from a text that contained derogatory terms for Latinos and African Americans. The mentor noted that she was appalled that the teacher used this in the classroom: "She feels it's fine and has just given me the full excerpt to read. I have yet to read it, but our conversation was disturbing to me. She felt it was fine because Latinos were calling each other names." The mentor faced challenges in balancing the delicate nature of maintaining trust with the beginning teacher, firmly confronting racist language and its impact on students, and exploring the pedagogical responsibility of teachers when using material of this nature.

Mentors were also confronted with the daunting duties of novices, often causing mentors to leave addressing issues of race until "classroom management was in place." Some mentors struggled to help new teachers make connections between classroom management and racial equality. Challenges emerging from mentors' responses were not unique. They echo findings of others who have surveyed other largely white teaching populations that have been socialized away from thinking about structural racism. As Sleeter notes in teaching whites about racism, "While denying structural racism, whites usually spend their lives in white-dominated spheres, constructing an understanding of race and social equality from that vantage point" (1998, p. 37). I would add that the very nature of schooling results in this denial of structural racism among some educators of color also, despite their own lived experience of racism.

A PROFESSIONAL DEVELOPMENT INITIATIVE ON ANTIRACIST MENTORING

Based on themes from mentors' writings and on work I had developed over two decades, I designed and facilitated a professional development series entitled *Making Equity Explicit*. Its goal was to further develop skills, knowledge, and attitudes of new teacher mentors to recognize and address inequities in classrooms, schools, and teacher practice, with a particular focus on race, language, and culture. I entitled this professional development initiative *Making Equity Explicit* because of the vague way in which equity tends to be spoken about in many educational circles. One central feature of my work as a professional developer is sharing with participants the vision of equity in teaching and learning I have developed, specifically that equity-centered practice

- Embraces positive development of the student's identity as an essential aspect of teaching and learning
- Validates knowledge that is frequently omitted from the curriculum
- Redistributes a wide range of skills among those who have traditionally not had access to them
- Nurtures positive attitudes toward struggles for social justice and equality
- Ensures equitable educational outcomes for students from all social groups
- References communities that have been excluded from discussion and decisionmaking
- Celebrates cultures of marginalized people

Building on this vision and on the mentors' specific strengths and challenges, I designed and facilitated an eight-session series over 2 years.

Goals

Learning goals throughout these sessions spoke directly to mentors' self-assessment and were embedded within professional standards for which they were held accountable. For example, in the first session, learning goals allowed mentors to build on work they had done on culture with ELLs and extend their repertoire to address the question of race in coaching conversations. They were to (1) develop a common language about race, culture, and equity; (2) explore ways their experiences of race and racism influence their perceptions and practice; and (3) practice raising issues of race and culture in their role as mentors. By the 2nd year of the professional development initiative, learning goals were directly linked to the California Standards for the Teaching Profession (CSTP): (1) examine the equity implications for the CSTP dealing with understanding and organizing subject matter for student learning; (2) practice coaching strategies to assist beginning teachers to build on student life experiences and prior knowledge to make the content meaningful and relevant; (3) identify cultural and racial biases in the curriculum; and (4) share strategies about home visits and building relationships with parents.

Processes

Highlighting the historical and institutional perspective. In approaching the challenge of the invisibility of race and its institutional nature, we looked at the history of legislation and official decisionmaking in public education and how legislation has privileged and continues to privilege groups

based on race, class, culture and language, and so forth. We also looked at
the legacy of legislation in our classrooms today and the need to address it
in our work as educators. One particular example proved to be a graphic
eye-opener to many participants. The *Historical Timeline of Public Educa-*
tion in the U.S. (Applied Research Center, 2001), one of the tools used for
this historical journey, states that in 1864,

> Congress makes it illegal for Native Americans to be taught in their native lan-
> guages. Native children as young as four years old are taken from their parents
> and sent to Bureau of Indian Affairs (BIA) off-reservation boarding schools, whose
> goal, as one BIA official put it, is to "kill the Indian to save the man." (p. 3)

Through this example, we explored the role of schooling in terms of "as-
similation" or "cultural genocide," depending on one's perspective. It also
led to some tense discussions and debates about the school's and teacher's
response to today's ELLs and their communities' languages.

Connected to this discussion were some effective approaches for supporting ELLs and other students of color to acquire knowledge and skills necessary to succeed in the larger society, while maintaining pride in their cultural
heritage and using their learning for self-determination of the cultural, racial,
and linguistic communities from which they came. These conversations were
sometimes characterized by defensiveness and other strong emotions, which
became part of the subject matter from which we gained insight into historical and institutional roots of racism. Specifically, we focused on the fact that
a new teacher who was not valuing a student's home language or culture was
not simply acting out of a matter of personal prejudice. Rather, such an attitude had a historical and institutional basis. The process of change therefore
had to include both individual attitude and the written and unwritten institutional policy that supported individual behavior.

Identifying social group membership. We engaged in activities to introduce and make operational the importance of identifying social group
membership. We examined the role played by class, gender, and racial and
cultural membership in our experiences as educators and as members of society. One such activity, entitled *Personal Cultural Racial History*, invited
participants to recall through drawings an early memory of race (Okazawa-
Rey, 1998, p. 65). In debriefing this activity, participants were struck by
commonalities and differences their colleagues had experienced along racial
lines. We came to realize that our story was not just our individual story but
also about how questions of power, privilege, advantage, or disadvantage
associated with our societal location impacted our opportunities and perspectives. Coupled with this insight was the challenge to work from both

social group membership and organizational location to make change toward equity in our respective sites. At each session, mentors reported on their successes and challenges as they had attempted to support new teachers.

Undertaking and expanding one's role as a change agent. This aspect of the professional development initiative was to expand the mentors' repertoire in raising issues of race. One approach to this process was through the use of a tool, *The Four A's*. The A's refer to *awareness, action, analysis,* and *attitude change.* I developed this tool to address a tendency to focus on changing attitude without appropriate attention to some of the antecedents of attitude change. Raising awareness, identifying ways to act on that awareness, and analyzing outcomes of the action seem to be important factors in changing attitude. One of the areas of awareness is with respect to social group membership or social location. For example, what are the implications of a white teacher mentor who is working with a new teacher born in India and wondering whether her culture "was getting in the way of communication with parents"? We discussed various awareness issues to be addressed in this case.

Applying the equity principle in teaching, mentoring, and leadership. The "equity principle" came to be understood as the practice of undertaking measures necessary to undo or redress inequities in teaching, mentoring, and other aspects of schooling in order to ensure that everyone experiences equality. The equity/equality formula is as follows: Equity is the process. Equality is the goal. To achieve this goal, a range of resources including reflective activities, tools, professional readings, and audiovisual materials were used throughout the series. A typical opening activity was as follows: "Think of an example when you would say you were intentionally teaching or mentoring for equity. Identify the inequality you were attempting to address. Share your experience with others at your table." Such an activity produced concrete examples from lives of new teachers and mentors and also allowed us to deepen our knowledge of ways in which inequality plays out in schools (e.g., patterns of suspension along race lines).

A reflection tool entitled *Checking My Systems for Equity* was a central resource in our work (Lee, 2001). Mentors included this reflective tool in both coaching and observation aspects of their work. New teachers used it for self-reflection. It consists of eight segments devoted to the planning, instructing, and reflecting aspects of teaching and learning. For each segment, the new teacher and/or mentor write reflectively on a domain of concern. This is not a summative assessment tool or a checklist to be ticked off. Rather, mentors can invite new teachers to reflect on various aspects of their students' social identity and the prior knowledge they would bring into the room when planning lessons for those students. For example, a teacher during the preparation stage would ask: "Which students in terms of gender, culture, race, language, immigration status, and class can relate to these learning goals, activities, and this material?" Closely connected to awareness of students' background is the nature of the learning tasks and their goals in terms of students' learning. Thus the next set of reflective questions asks: "How can I include a range of tasks to engage the realities of experiences in the room?" or "How can I link this lesson to the multiple ways in which students' knowledge will be assessed?"

In the instructing phase of the work, new teachers would be encouraged to reflect on aspects of their work dealing with teacher talk, attention, tone, and direction and, in turn, student talk and participation. Some of the reflective questions in this section include: "What language am I using to check for understanding among various groups of learners?" and "How much am I talking in comparison to the amount of time students are talking?" In the final section, items are related to the learning that can occur after a lesson has been taught and the teacher uses questions to see how she or he can refine her or his practice. These questions expand from reflections related to insights gained from examining student work, to insights gained from talking with students, parents, and other colleagues.

Another resource we tapped was sample lessons that promoted antiracist content and pedagogy. Lessons included a wide range of subjects, from mathematics to art. While students learned how to find the median or to work with percentages as required by district math standards, they were also able to see how mathematics was a tool for exploring economic inequities. They would examine the median weekly earnings of full-time workers in various professions by gender, race, and ethnic origin (see samples in Lee, Menkart, & Okazawa-Rey, 1998). We also viewed videos to analyze antiracist teaching. For example, *Reflections* (Outlook, 1996) features teachers demonstrating how to support students to identify racial bias in texts.

Role-play exercises based on experiences of mentors and new teachers, and aligned with professional standards, provided further learning opportunities. One role-play prompt that focused on creating and maintaining effective environments for student learning read: "I am a new teacher with a lot to think about, classroom management etc. . . . I think I'm going to put off multicultural education until my second year." Mentors participating in this role-play enacted a coaching conversation that would support the new teacher in making the connection between classroom management, multicultural environments, and the significance of such a climate for students from a range of cultural backgrounds. In another role-play focused on understanding and organizing subject matter for student learning, mentors played out responses to the following new teacher questions: "How can I bring different cultural perspectives in a class like Math? Besides, I've only one black student in my class."

POCKETS OF PROMISE

While it is difficult to claim direct causal effects of this professional development initiative, I highlight below four changes or "pockets of promise" that mentors reported were the result of their participation in this work.

First, participants reported growth in their consciousness of self and social group membership. One respondent wrote, "I have learned about myself as a person, a teacher, a mentor and in general, how that comes across to others. I have heightened awareness of how that affects my work." Another noted the insight gained at "so many levels—personal, social, historical, and intellectual, and how to bring these new understandings into the day-day-day work of education from the teacher to the institution."

Second, participants described the development of their capacities and strategies for equity-focused mentoring. For example, one respondent reflected, "I've had a huge increase in awareness of what to observe in classrooms in terms of curriculum/subject matter as well as teacher/student and student/student interactions." Another identified, "I've learned to look at curriculum in light of what voices are missing and whose perspectives are missing."

Third, mentors began to recognize their role as agents of change. One stated, "I have learned not to be afraid to bring up important issues around racism." Another mentor explained the importance of taking action: "Intentions have less impact than actions. It isn't enough to say that you don't notice differences among your students. More important is to consider what may be a lack-of-equity issue for them that you didn't see coming."

Finally, some mentors pinpointed greater ability to make equity explicit in their coaching. One respondent wrote, "As mentors, we are better able to recognize opportunities for making new teachers aware of equity issues they can influence." Another wrote, "In my work with novices, I will be focusing our conversations on equity issues as a matter of course, having equity be an underlying structure for planning."

REFLECTIONS AND RECOMMENDATIONS

Not all of the mentors experienced the professional development in such positive ways. The response of one participant highlights the dilemma I face as a professional development consultant of antiracist education. This mentor reported conducting personal research that yielded a different perspective. This individual found my view of culture misguided and my views of race shortsighted, noting that my approach to equity was polarizing and separatist without improving the socioeconomic conditions for minorities. After two decades of providing professional development in antiracist education, I have learned the number one rule of not regarding evaluations as personal attacks. I employed this rule in response to the above evaluation and drew from it the following lessons. First, the series was not presented in such a doctrinaire manner as to leave this participant feeling that there was only one right answer to the questions posed. Second, it inspired this participant to conduct her/his own research. Third, the already polarized nature of this country along the lines of race was not made convincingly enough for this participant. Finally, work on race, education, and mentoring can still be viewed as highly untheorized and thus may be reduced to "a matter of opinion" in ways that would not be true for other areas of study.

Besides such challenges as that mentor's comments, others assume they have completed their work on equity once the series is ended. While having only scratched the surface of equity issues, it is still easy to leave participants with a sense that they are "done" focusing on the area of equity. A further dilemma is embedded in the fact that having done the series, the organization has very high expectations of the competencies that have been developed. It is expected that participants will take up equity issues at every turn. We know that professional development, alone without more dramatic systemic change, will not alter an organization.

Despite emotional bumps on the way, I still feel excitement from the opportunity to look back on the experience of *Making Equity Explicit.* Many features of mentors' organizational context, mentors' own willingness to grow, and the opportunity to debrief and plan with co-facilitators contributed significantly to the pockets of promise that emerged. That excitement is tempered, however, when I consider the ideological tidal wave of specious meritocracy and denial of racial inequality that must be confronted in all educational work if equity is to be achieved. *Making Equity Explicit* is one attempt to move in the direction of educational equality. I offer these recommendations for induction leaders and mentors in continuing this work:

1. Hire more mentors and teachers of color in order to provide a wider range of perspectives and human experiences within the organization.
2. Work to create an organizational climate in which perspectives reflecting the life experiences from people of color can become an integral part of the organization.

3. Continue professional development that enables all members of the organization to make equity explicit in all aspects of planning, policy, and professional development.
4. Create the expectation between new teachers and mentors that issues of equity and race will be discussed and acted upon, and that such discussions/actions are essential parts of the coaching relationship.
5. Build expectations of the evidence of equity in all aspects of the organization's work.

REFERENCES

Applied Research Center. (2001). *Historical timeline of public education in the U.S.* Retrieved June 24, 2003, from http://ww.arc.org/erase/jtimeline.html

Lee, E. (2001). *Checking my systems for equity.* Retrieved June 24, 2004, from www.enidlee.com

Lee, E., Menkart, D., & Okazawa-Rey, M. (Eds.). (1998). *Beyond heroes and holidays: A practical guide to K–12 anti-racist, multicultural education and staff development.* Washington, DC: Teaching for Change.

Okazawa-Rey, M. (1998). Personal cultural history exercise. In E. Lee, D. Menkart, & M. Okazawa-Rey (Eds.), *Beyond heroes and holidays: A practical guide to K–12 anti-racist, multicultural education and staff development* (pp. 65–66). Washington, DC: Teaching for Change.

Outlook (Producer). (1996). *Reflections* (video). Ontario Ministry of Training and Education. Available from the Metropolitan School Board, School Programs and Services, 45 York Mills Rd., North York, Ontario, Canada M2P 1B6, (416) 397-2509.

Sleeter, C. (1998). Teaching whites about racism. In E. Lee, D. Menkart, & M. Okazawa-Rey (Eds.), *Beyond heroes and holidays: A practical guide to K–12 anti-racist, multicultural education and staff development* (pp. 36–44) Washington, DC: Teaching for Change.

PART II

A Mentor's Knowledge of Curriculum and Teaching

What should mentors know and be able to do in relation to curriculum and teaching? Mentors need a depth of knowledge about how and what to teach students and about how and what to teach and do in guiding and developing novice teachers. The chapters in this part explore four areas of curriculum and teaching that are both promising and deeply problematic for mentors: (1) a pedagogy of *coaching conversations* that is educative for new teachers; (2) *subject-matter*–specific mentoring; (3) *tailoring mentor development* to local and individual needs; and (4) implementing a *curriculum* of mentor professional development. Collectively these chapters address complexities and promising practices in mentors' knowledge of *what* and *how* to teach novices.

In Chapter 4, Lori Helman examines the complexity of a mentor's pedagogy of coaching conversations. She explores what occurs in a mentoring conference and how the coaching stance a mentor takes in this exchange shapes the new knowledge and capacities the novice teacher can develop, particularly in ways that foster reflection and learning. The chapter examines mentor–novice conferences for moves that mentors make and ways these utterances do or do not appear to have an impact on novices' responses. From her analyses, Helman generates a model curriculum for mentor professional development.

In Chapter 5, Athanases et al. consider cases of mentors in new positions as mentor leaders who must determine appropriate curriculum for development of mentors. These leaders confront the tension of using forms, scripts, and routines to support mentor development while also needing to adapt such scaffolds to local needs and to monitor their usefulness. The chapter highlights principles and ideas relevant to mentors who may face similar challenges of designing mentor curriculum that provides professional support while attending to local needs.

In Chapter 6, Linda Shore and Laura Stokes report on work conducted at San Francisco's Exploratorium, the world-renowned hands-on museum of science, which also supports a dynamic community of science teachers. This chapter contributes to conceptualizing the knowledge base of mentors by featuring subject matter content and expertise in the work of mentoring new teachers. Shore and Stokes examine practices of veteran teachers of science working with new teachers to help them build classroom practice: designing science lessons and units, managing students during hands-on inquiry experiences, and finding and using the "stuff" of science. The chapter reflects on science-specific mentoring of new teachers as a means of cultivating and renewing a discipline-based teacher professional community.

In Chapter 7, Barbara Davis argues the critical significance of a curriculum for professional development of mentors and provides examples of field-tested practices. She explores dimensions of the curriculum for mentor development, including formative assessment of novices, support strategies of mentors, and mentor self-assessment. Davis identifies rationales and strategies mentors and induction leaders have used successfully for mentor development.

CHAPTER 4

What's in a Conversation? Mentoring Stances in Coaching Conferences and How They Matter

Lori Helman

Tracy's concerns surface even as I put down my bag and join her at the table. "I'm really concerned about my students' progress in reading. I don't know what to do." I agree with her concern, but I decide not to say that her students do need more guidance in small groups. How can I guide her without imposing? She sits upright like a tree that has survived its first winter but does not yet have girth or heavy bark. "Let's talk about your thinking so far." Two questions circulate in my mind as I frame this mentoring conversation.[1] How do I phrase my comments and questions to help her grow in her own ability to problem-solve? How will I ensure that when I leave this discussion she has better ability to set explicit literacy goals in her classroom?

In this anecdote from my own practice as a mentor, there exists a tension between passing on the teaching knowledge gained through experience and promoting the autonomy, creativity, and self-reflection of the novice. In order to truly be transformational, our induction programs must both equip beginning teachers with tools for best practice, and develop the disposition in beginning teachers to think deeply about and contextualize these practices to meet the needs of their individual students.

The following study comes from the work of one beginning teacher induction program to refine the "curriculum of mentoring"—the skills, attitudes, and procedures new teacher mentors use in order to support novice learning and reflection. We wondered how these mentors might extend and deepen the thinking of the beginning teacher within a coaching conversation. In the cases presented here, we examine the language and techniques mentors used in mentoring conferences. We describe how these skills are applied, and we investigate their appropriateness. Those who currently run an induction program, or are considering implementing one, will be interested in learning more about the skills outlined here that mentors need. New teacher mentors will find that these case studies provide examples of practice to analyze and compare to their own work. Classroom teachers may use these examples to think about how to structure collaborative interactions with colleagues, as well as how these ideas may apply to structuring environments for student learning and reflection.

INVESTIGATING MENTORING CONVERSATIONS

This work is drawn from the Santa Cruz New Teacher Project (SCNTP), a well-established program for beginning teacher support and assessment that began in 1988. The SCNTP releases exemplary teachers full-time to mentor a caseload of new teachers. Each year a cadre of new mentors joins the SCNTP staff. Just as the range of needs varies in a classroom of students and a group of new teachers, so, too, does the range of mentor needs. One goal of this study was to examine data for how a mentor contributes to novice development. Another was to guide us in creating research-informed professional development.

The research team included six mentors with at least 4 years of mentoring experience each.[2] These team members were leaders in the SCNTP and responsible for professional development for mentors. The research team met over a 2-year period to design a study and analyze the results. We examined a range of data from interactions of four mentor/new teacher pairs including tape recordings of pre- and post-conferences between new teacher and mentor related to a specific literacy lesson; videotapes of beginning teachers' literacy teaching; mentor notes of the lesson observation; student work samples; and beginning teacher collaborative logs. The four mentors in the study were released full-time to work with their beginning teachers and had participated in structured professional development on effective conferencing. Each of the new teachers was in her 1st year of teaching and taught in grades 2–5.

In subgroup partnerships, research team members listened to and transcribed audiotapes of coaching conversations. These conversations were then discussed with the whole team where deeper analysis led to discovery of common themes in mentoring behaviors. In the spring of 2001, we conducted a focus group of mentors that included those in the study. Participants were asked to reflect upon their use of mentoring strategies within coaching conversations. They were also asked to self-assess relating to mentoring skills needed. The research team examined focus group notes to identify needs mentioned and overarching themes.

THREE MENTORING STANCES

In the four case studies examined, mentors assumed several stances with new teachers. In coaching conversations, mentors alternately (1) probed to extend the beginning teacher's thinking, (2) explicitly taught or suggested a specific practice, or (3) focused the teacher on how the lesson was accountable to larger school and state standards (see Column 2 in Figure 4.1). Each of these practices is a critical skill in the mentor's repertoire. Each mentoring stance assumes that knowledge is located in one of three places: with new teachers, mentors, or institutions. When the mentor extends thinking, the core knowledge is assumed to reside in the new teacher. Teaching directly assumes that some important knowledge is located in the mentor. Promoting accountability locates important authority in the institutions. Of course, knowledge is never located only in one place, and in fact these areas are always interacting to greater or lesser degrees.

As we reviewed language of case study conversations, we found that the stance a mentor took in dialogue impacted the new teacher's reaction. For example, when a mentor asked more open-ended questions, novice responses were longer and more reflective. In data analysis that follows, I will look at each mentor stance and show examples of the specific language used in the case studies. I will describe what it looks like for a mentor to extend thinking, teach directly, or promote accountability. When do these actions occur? What else happens? I do not describe an idealized situation. As with teaching, coaching conversations are complex processes involving multiple opportunities for mentor decisionmaking and action. For this reason, I also analyze what a missed opportunity looks like—a time when it might have been more appropriate to use a different mentor stance. What do we observe in these cases, and what can we learn from them? Following the three stances, I discuss the importance that mentor stances have on developing a "curriculum of mentoring" in the professional development of mentors.

Figure 4.1. Analysis of Coaching Conversation

Assessment of New Teacher Needs	Mentor Stance Taken	Possible Mentor Actions Taken	Possible New Teacher Responses
New teacher has background knowledge of topic	Extend thinking	Clarifies, paraphrases, probes, makes connections, projects, or pauses to elicit possible solutions from new teacher	Examines personal experience, reflects, analyzes, creates, visualizes, brainstorms, bounces ideas off of mentor to formulate possible plan
New teacher lacks ideas, asks for help, or doesn't recognize the problem	Teach directly	Defines, suggests, tells, illustrates from own experience, shows how, explains why, or elaborates on to provide information to new teacher	Asks for clarification or greater explanation, requests modeling, accepts or rejects usefulness of idea, adapts new idea for personal use
Learning and/or teaching goals are not focused on systemic standards	Promote accountability	Questions, tells, researches, or problem-solves with the beginning teacher to identify applicable teaching or learning standards	Asks for clarification of standards and application to lesson, incorporates standards into plan to varying degrees

Extending Beginning Teacher Thinking

Once a mentor has ascertained that the new teacher has background knowledge concerning a topic (see Figure 4.1, Row 1), an appropriate stance may be to build on and extend the thinking of the novice. A mentor may use a variety of techniques to promote deeper thinking or elicit possible solutions from the new teacher during the coaching conversation. Drawing from our data, some of these techniques include:

- Using clarifying questions ("What do you mean by 'a good story'?")
- Paraphrasing ("So, you're saying that certain students get done faster than others?")
- Probing ("Tell me more about how you've done that before.")

- Making connections ("How does seating arrangement affect student behavior issues?")
- Projecting ("What might it look like to modify the work for your special-needs students?")
- Brainstorming ("What are some ways you have seen or heard of that being done?")
- Pausing (Leaving space in the conversation for the beginning teacher to think and speak.)

The following excerpt from a planning conference illustrates an example of extending thinking. The mentor helps the new teacher think about expectations for a story-writing project with 2nd-graders. (T = new teacher; M = mentor.)

T: The story itself is pretty unstructured. I haven't told them how long the story is. I'm a little unsure myself how long it should be.

M: Yeah, is there anything that says it in the book where it tells them to write a story? Is there anything from the book?

T: Umm, it talks about having a beginning, middle and end.

M: Um huh . . .

T: I don't see anything about how long it is.

M: When they did their district writing assessment, what came from them as far as length?

T: It's pretty much three sentences, and they are trying to go for a paragraph which is at least four.

M: In any other kinds of writing, have you seen anything beyond a few sentences in response?

T: Um, the high ones can do several sentences but the average is probably just three sentences in a response for a question or story.

M: So the idea that they are going to write a story with a beginning, middle, and end is going to be a leap for them at this point.

T: Okay.

M: Yeah, wouldn't you say?

T: Definitely. A big stretch.

In this example, we see the mentor using probing questions such as, "Is there anything from the book?" "Have you seen anything beyond a few sentences in response?" and "What came from them as far as length?" She also projects how this knowledge might affect the expectations for the lesson by stating, "So, the idea that they are going to write a story with a beginning, middle, and end is going to be a leap for them at this point." Following this section of the conversation, once the new teacher makes the connection between where the students are and what the task requires, the mentor guides her to set reasonable expectations and provide the scaffolding her 2nd-grade students will need.

In the next example we join a mentor and 2nd-grade teacher in a conference following a classroom observation. We note that although the mentor asks questions, she misses the opportunity to support the new teacher's extended thinking because she answers her own questions and does not provide the space for the novice to articulate her own reflections.

M: What were some of the things you remember doing? There were a few times when you'd ask a question and two hands were going up . . . Gloria and Valerie. I remember seeing you do a number of different things to . . . You could have just called on them, and maybe once or twice you did, but there were a number of things you did, do you remember what you did? To kind of spread it out.

T: Ummmm . . . I think I asked them to read it again to themselves on a few different occasions. When there are only two hands up, there's no point in saying, "Talk to a partner," because they're not going to be sharing information that's necessarily what I'm getting at. When more of them raise their hands, then, "Talk to the person next to you" is better . . .

M: So, that's a really good point that if only two people know it, "Talk to your partner" isn't going to work , and one thing you did do . . .

T: Yeah . . .

M: You did a couple of things. You asked the question, "What does it need? Does it sound good?" And they said, "Yes, great." So you went back and modeled, you read it really rapidly and you ran out of breath and then they got it. So one thing was that you modeled more. That was a way to get them to where you wanted them to go. I've been thinking, that's a teacher thought . . . kids talk in these long, long sentences and we're asking them to write in shorter sentences and you did the perfect thing—you modeled why.

T: Uh-hmmm . . .

M: You had them in pairs talking about how to make it better, and there was talking and it was hard to tell if it was on task. You modeled it and you circled all the "y"s and all of a sudden there were all these hands and people saying, "Put a period. Get rid of the 'y's." That was another time you modeled it and then participation went way up. And then there was a time when you were saying something is still lacking . . . and two hands went up, three hands up, and then you had them chorus-reading. Six hands went up and when they choral-read it you could hear because when they got to the end you could just hear it. A lot of times when it seemed not everyone had it, you went back and put in some more input. So, it was like you were saying . . . doing a partner share when they don't have enough input isn't going to do it. You circled it, you had them read it, you modeled it.

The mentor does a comprehensive job of summarizing and analyzing what she saw the teacher do in the lesson. Because of the volume of mentor talk, however, there is little time or support for the new teacher to do her own reflection.

Direct Teaching During a Coaching Conversation

At a given point in the coaching conversation a mentor may become aware that the beginning teacher lacks important information about a key area being discussed (see Figure 4.1, Row 2). This awareness may develop from the questions the mentor has been asking, when the strategy of extending thinking has reached a standstill, or when a new teacher specifically asks for help. During direct teaching the mentor relays big ideas or discrete skills that the new teacher does not yet possess. Both explicit subject matter knowledge and context-based instructional strategies are shared. In direct teaching, we have observed that the mentor may:

- Define a concept ("Reciprocal reading is a process in which . . .")
- Make a suggestion ("Taking a stretch break may work well at that point in the lesson.")
- Tell ("What I know about working with second language learners is . . .")
- Illustrate from own experience ("When I organized a class field trip I structured groups by . . .")
- Show how ("Here's how I might write up a language experience group chart.")
- Elaborate on ("You mentioned ____, one additional idea relating to that is _____")
- Explain why ("Doing a quick check for understanding with your students is one way to get an assessment of whether your class is ready to move on, or if the topic needs further explanation.")

In the following example, a mentor uses direct teaching during a planning conference so that students will face fewer unfamiliar tasks during an upcoming lesson.

M: I want to say something about the student sharing. That's a really
nice idea to get them to verbalize what they want to write before
they write it because it will be bringing up a lot more language
than if you just start writing. That file folder in their head has
been opened. It's also a nice addition to cooperative learning
strategies.

T: Yeah, we're still trying to work on that . . .

M: And you will . . . you might want to think about doing it in pairs.
It might even be good to use stable pairs. That's a structure they
know already.

T: So always use the same people?

M: You may want to change but I was thinking that this sharing
pictures and talking about a beginning, middle, and end, and this
whole writing process is a big stretch from where they are right
now with writing. And since that is a very challenging task, give
them a cooperative structure they are comfortable with.

T: Umm, okay.

M: Rather than giving this new cognitive task—beginning, middle,
and end—and a new cooperative task, sharing at the table with
four people.

T: Yeah, it sounds like it would help them be more successful.

M: Maybe . . . Yeah, think about the real focus.

In the above conversation, the mentor elaborates on a strategy the new teacher
has mentioned. She then makes a suggestion and explains why changing both
the task and the organizational structure of the lesson may be too much to
ask of the 2nd-grade students.

Mentors at times may miss opportunities to supply new teachers with
vital information. In the following conversation, the new teacher realizes there
might be problems moving desks.

M: Okay . . . and what about the new teaching strategy, do you feel
comfortable with "Round Table" after reading the instructions
of how to get them into groups?

T: Right, right.

M: Are you going to move any furniture?

T: I think I'm going to have this table and a front table. I need the
students to face each other and be comfortable. That might mean
we'll have a transition of moving. Well, I could have the furniture already moved in the morning when they come in. However,
moving it back would be an interesting transition. Do you have
an idea?

M: Yeah. Well . . .
T: I could seat them on the floor.
M: That might be hard for writing.
T: Exactly.
M: I wonder what it would look like if you . . . you have a few days before you actually do the lesson.
T: Right.

The mentor questions the new teacher and tries to build on her background knowledge, but is reluctant to offer direct advice. In the end, the novice's request to get help in managing the movement of furniture for the proposed lesson is left unsatisfied.

Promoting Accountability in the Coaching Conversation

Professional standards for teachers and content standards for students are currently forefront in the educational landscape. During the course of any coaching conversation, and especially in a planning conference, the mentor typically will check to see that the novice's goals are based on systemic teaching and learning standards (Figure 4.1, Row 3). For instance, if a new teacher is working on development of her teaching skills, the mentor may help her find an appropriate professional teaching standard (such as those contained in the California Standards for the Teaching Profession, 1996) on which to focus. With any content-based lesson, the mentor may help the novice to identify grade-level content standards to work toward in the lesson. The use of systemic standards helps meet institutional expectations for performance located within the context of the novice's teaching environment. As indicated earlier, in a sense this mentor stance locates authority in neither the teacher nor the mentor but in the institution that has articulated standards. In this stance, the mentor may engage in extending thinking or in direct instruction about a standard, but the stance involves looking together at how the novice's work can be shaped by and aligned with standards.

A mentor may promote accountability by:

- Questioning ("What teaching standard would you like me to observe for when I come in tomorrow?")
- Telling ("The 4th-grade writing standard includes ____.")
- Researching ("I'll get a copy of the Math Framework so we can look up the geometry expectations for 6th grade.")
- Problem-solving with the new teacher ("Where can we find your school's expectations for implementing the fall writing performance assessment?")

In the following example of promoting accountability, the mentor questions her new teacher about evidence of 4th graders' success in the lesson.

> M: How are you going to determine, what's the evidence that
>   students have achieved results?
> T: This is what I've been thinking about. I don't know if they need to
>   do another sample to see if students utilized past tense in a
>   correct way or what. The pre-evidence was the writing sample. I
>   don't know if I should do another one at the end of the lesson on
>   the following day.
> M: Yeah, it sounds like that would be really interesting evidence.
> T: Right.
> M: You've got your first set. Then you could look at them side by
>   side.
> T: And really see. That's what I was thinking would be authentic.

In the above scenario, the mentor builds on the new teacher's sense of importance in using student work to show progress. Questions about evidence of student success promote accountability for teaching in relation to assessed student needs.

The following example illustrates a situation in which mentor and novice do not come to an agreement about a plan for the proposed organization of a lesson. Rather, the teaching strategy is left ambiguous. In this case, the mentor has been discussing whether students will be at desks or in the circle. The mentor suggests the circle.

> M: Does that sound doable? So, this is something you might think
>   about tonight. And think about your S.F.A. [Success for All
>   reading program] structures and think about if that feels natural
>   for you, because I want it to feel really like it's going to flow for
>   you. I know you've had performance experience with your
>   summer school. I know you've done performance, and so think
>   back to how did that work for you in that setting. And if it was
>   more conducive to pull them away from desks, then let's think
>   about that.
> T: All right.
> M: It sounds like that might be the best way to go.

In a situation such as this, it is unclear if the new teacher knows how to proceed. In this case, referring to teaching standards may have been useful to help focus the teacher and provide a structure for setting a goal. For example, the mentor might have suggested thinking about the state *Standard for Creating and Maintaining Effective Environments for Student Learning.* One component of that standard asks teachers to think about how they arrange and adapt classroom seating to accommodate individual and group learning needs. Examining the standard together could lead to clarifying what seating would be most appropriate in the lesson context.

Summary

In the above findings, we note several overarching ideas:

1. Structured conversations between a mentor and a novice provide a powerful opportunity for supporting reflective thinking, teaching specific content and instructional practices, and incorporating an understanding of expectations for teaching and learning in the classroom.
2. The coaching conversation is a complex event, which includes numerous opportunities for the mentor to vary his or her stance depending on a variety of circumstances.
3. Specific behaviors and language accompany taking on a certain mentoring stance.
4. The stance a mentor adopts impacts the amount of thinking and reflection a novice does in the coaching conversation, as well as the scope of issues a teacher considers.

Participants' Reflections

Following analysis of the coaching conversations, we invited mentors who participated in the study to attend a focus group discussion to share their insights. Focus group data revealed that mentors appear more comfortable describing when to use a specific mentoring strategy, rather than how or why to use it. In addition, they shared that their relationship with a new teacher and the new teacher's emotional state played a role in deciding which mentoring stance to use. Mentors wondered if the direct teaching stance occurred more often when a mentor was working in his or her subject matter of expertise. Such an observation holds important implications. Mentors stated that external expectations (such as student performance objectives, teacher evaluation methods, and induction program procedures) increased the level of accountability addressed in the coaching conversation. Another key idea expressed by mentors in the focus group was that participating in the research study was very meaningful and enriched their mentoring practices.

TOWARD A MODEL OF CURRICULUM FOR MENTORS

Coaching conversations provide varied opportunities for mentors to assist novices in moving teaching practice forward. By assuming a stance of extending thinking, direct teaching, or promoting accountability, the mentor impacts a new teacher's learning and reflection. Specific behaviors associated with these stances do not necessarily come automatically to mentors; because of the complexity of this conferencing event, there are many skills and ideas that might be included in a professional development plan to support mentor learning.

This study is a case of mentors looking in depth at specific language and behaviors of coaching conversations with new teachers. With the lens focused intensely on this aspect of our work, and the time set aside to collaboratively reflect on what it meant, we gained perspectives on complexities of how mentors support new teacher growth in our New Teacher Project. The ultimate goal of our study was to learn how to better structure professional development to develop skills and dispositions of effective mentoring. In the meantime, our ongoing discussions helped the researchers become better mentors for new teachers with whom we worked.

We discovered that when a mentor wants to encourage a new teacher's reflection and extended thinking, he or she should use clarifying, paraphrasing, probing, making connections, projecting, brainstorming, and pausing. When a novice has limited knowledge or experience, a more appropriate stance would be to share professional knowledge, complete with the whys and hows. In most coaching conferences it also is appropriate to bring in systemic expectations so that the work in induction is aligned with expectations of the institution in which support is located.

Given that coaching conversations are powerful and complex tools for mentors in their work with new teachers, it is clear that to make the most of their use, mentors will need many opportunities to learn about, discuss, try out, and reflect upon how these conversations are put into practice. If we as mentors can impact the course of the conference through the stance we take, what are examples of the language and behavior that can support our work at specific points in the conversation? What contexts are appropriate for extending thinking, teaching directly, or promoting accountability? These questions must be addressed explicitly as we support mentor development.

Our analysis of both the transcripts of coaching conversations and the mentor focus group meeting helped us identify many of the circumstances that play into the choice of stance taken during a conference. In Figure 4.2, we examine various factors and the impact these areas may have for mentor professional development.

Figure 4.2. Toward a Model of Curriculum for Mentors

Factor Affecting Mentor Stance Taken	Area of Possible Professional Development for Mentors
Relationship with new teacher	Interpersonal relationships (knowing how to establish trust, build relationships)
New teacher state of mind	"Reading" a beginning teacher's emotional state
Level of knowledge base of new teacher	Assessing the new teacher's knowledge base in a skill or topic
Purpose of the conference	Understanding the purpose of various coaching conferences (planning, postobservation reflection, analysis of student work, etc.)
External expectations	Knowing grade-level content and performance standards for students, professional teaching standards, and purposes and procedures of the induction program in which mentor operates

Supporting the mentor to refine his or her skills in using the various stances will take explicit intent, time, and practice. Effective professional development provides opportunities for mentors to see examples, role-play, discuss, analyze, try out, and get feedback on the language, behavior, and contextual implementation of each mentor stance. Our research team learned about mentoring by analyzing case study conversations, serving as a model itself of professional development. Reference materials and ways of documenting conversations support mentors' work and their structuring of coaching conversations. These may include collaborative reflection logs, planning and reflecting conference protocols, and analysis of student work formats. With continual feedback from mentors and novices, tools can be used and revised to support thoughtful implementation of coaching conversations. If mentors need other resource materials or structures, these also can be developed.

This study confirmed our belief that mentoring is a complex activity. We looked at one part of the job—facilitating a coaching conversation. Within that piece we pulled out mentor stances, language, and behaviors that need to be developed and supported in mentors. Clearly, one cannot simply pull veteran teachers out of the classroom, call them mentors, and expect them to have the skills needed to handle this complex work. We have identified that it seems to be difficult for some mentors to know when to extend novice thinking and when to teach more directly—issues that can inform future professional development.

This study contributes to an understanding of what effective mentoring practices and professional development for mentors look like. If we hope to build a competent, committed, and reflective teaching force to carry our schools forward, it will require exemplary mentoring programs. Induction program leaders at all levels—local, regional, state, and national—need to understand deeply what it means to mentor. Policymakers who understand roles the mentor plays and the complexity of the skills needed will help create systems that validate and support structures for mentor learning. Teaching and learning are complicated whether they happen in a classroom or in a coaching conversation between two adults. There is often not an easy answer to the question of whether to probe, to reflect, or to explicitly teach. Human relationships always add a dimension that defies mathematical certainty. However, with a sense of what mentor stances are and why they are important, we can become clearer about when and how they can be applied, and what they can yield.

NOTES

1. Although the terms may suggest different meanings, I use mentoring conversation and coaching conference interchangeably in this chapter.
2. Members of our LNTI team—Wendy Baron, Rain Bongolan, Marney Cox, Jan Miles, and Leslie Smith—all contributed to the topics discussed in this chapter.

REFERENCES

California Department of Education/California Commission on Teacher Credentialing. (1996). *California standards for the teaching profession.* Sacramento: California Department of Education.
Success for All. Baltimore, MD: Success for All Foundation.

CHAPTER 5

Adopt, Adapt, Invent: Induction Leaders Designing Mentor Curriculum

*Steven Z. Athanases,
with Jennifer Abrams, Gordon Jack,
Virginia Johnson, Susan Kwock,
Judy McCurdy, Suzi Riley,
and Susan Totaro*

As mentors assume leadership of mentor programs, what kind of mentoring curriculum should they use? Should externally developed resources be adopted? How should they be adapted to local needs of students, teachers, mentors, and induction program? Or should new curriculum be invented? This chapter considers cases of mentors in new positions as mentor leaders who must determine appropriate curriculum for mentor development. These leaders confront the tension of using forms, scripts, and routines to support mentor development while needing also to adapt such scaffolds to local needs and to monitor their usefulness. Drawing on four cases of induction leadership from the Leadership Network for Teacher Induction (LNTI, see Introduction), we map a continuum of ways programs have assumed control of mentor curriculum—from adopting entire programs, to adapting materials to local needs, and on to inventing programs for particular contexts.

THE TENSION OF GENERIC SUPPORTS
AND TAILORED FOCUS

LNTI case studies reveal a recurring tension between values of and need for structures and routines to scaffold mentor learning and practice and, on the other hand, a need to adapt these scaffolds to local needs and to monitor their usefulness. As more experienced others, we often teach those less experienced by using what Vygotsky called scaffolds, structures that approximate learning outcomes and that can be dismantled as they grow unnecessary for the learner. Mothers as primary caregivers were observed breaking down tasks into doable parts. Teaching a child to tie shoelaces meant teaching first how to make a loop with one lace, then a loop with another, then how to bring them together into a tie. Educational psychologists adapted this theory of scaffolding among mothers and children to one of instructional scaffolding (e.g., Wood, Bruner, & Ross, 1976), providing a model for teachers to anticipate difficulties of learning tasks and to design appropriate supports.

Problems arise in instructional scaffolding, however. Scaffolds get designed for generic groups, often losing sensitivity to individuals and their contexts. One might ask:

* Scaffolding for whom, when, and in what context?
* Should teachers use the same scaffolds for all students?
* Should teacher educators use the same scaffolds for preservice teachers with different student populations?
* Should mentors use the same mentoring curriculum for novices with very different learning needs and degrees of engagement?
* Should mentor leaders use the same mentoring routine for new and more veteran mentors?

A challenge of scaffolds is that they can become reified, eclipsing concepts they were meant to teach, and insensitive to local and particular needs.

As we learn about effective curriculum for new teacher mentors, we pool understandings and work toward larger-scale means of educating a mentor force. In doing so, we face the same scaffolding dilemmas of all educators. First, are the guidelines, tools, and procedures we develop, share, and take to scale serving local needs, or do they interfere with education by remaining inflexible to local concerns? Second, how much structure do mentors need as adult learners developing knowledge and practice as mentors? If we fail to provide such structure, we neglect to see the mentor development context as a real learning situation. If we provide practical tools in mentor development, can we monitor their use so that forms do not swamp the work and steal the focus?

By curriculum, we refer first to *materials, resources, and artifacts* of instruction. In mentor development, this may include manuals, handouts, guidelines of mentoring procedures, and practical tools to guide mentoring work. Second, we refer to *activities* that occupy educational time. In mentor curriculum these include experiences a program encourages mentors to engage in as they mentor new teachers. Do these include in-class observations or merely after-school check-in chats? Do they include collaborative analysis of student work or merely cursory review of lesson plans? Activities include what mentors do at professional development sessions. These may be lecture presentations from leaders and outside experts. Sessions also may include activities to engage mentors in active learning—workshops, collaborative planning sessions, and role-playing of mentor/new teacher conversations. They even may include inquiry-oriented activities, such as action research cycles that invite mentors to ask critical questions of their own practice and to collect and analyze data that ultimately impact the nature of their work.

Finally, we consider the *hidden curriculum*, issues related to purposes for instruction, ideas, and underlying values that lessons promulgate, messages that get sent by what is and is not considered in a program's materials and lessons. In mentor programs, this can refer to program conceptions, stated or unstated, of what mentoring means and the purposes it serves. It also may refer to underlying conceptions of knowledge needed to mentor new teachers. If one believes that mentoring can be codified concisely and taught as routine practice, then a transmission model might guide development. This means that lectures, handouts, and formulaic activities may anchor mentor curriculum. If mentoring is cast primarily as helping novices adapt to local school norms, then mentor development will feature instruction in how to help new teachers fit in and not "rock the boat." On the other hand, if a program values critical perspectives on schools and believes that mentors hold potential to guide new teachers to be change agents making schools better serve all students, parents, and teachers, then mentor development may include attention to how to foster such critical stances. If a program values teacher reflection as a central tenet, creating continua of mentors engaged in reflection on their own practice and fostering such reflection in new teachers may take focus (Gaston, Wilson, & Davis, 2001). How, then, does an induction leader select materials and resources, development activities, and underlying purposes for mentor development, and with what degree of structure and support?

This chapter considers the power and limitations of forms, scripts, and routines in mentor curriculum. In cases we consider, members of an induction program team participated, through LNTI, in ongoing professional development related to program leadership and engaged in action research cycles. Case studies used a range of data sources, including interviews with mentors, new teachers, and administrators; focus groups of mentors; surveys of mentors and new teachers; field notes of meetings and classroom observations; records of mentor professional development sessions; and notes on informal exchanges and after-school "coffee talks." Steven participated in workshops and summer institutes with LNTI, guiding data analysis and writing of case studies. Together we analyzed what was important about these cases. In this chapter, we distill the cases into brief summaries, then glean principles and ideas relevant to wider audiences of mentors who may face similar challenges of designing mentor curriculum that provides professional support while attending to local needs and monitoring the usefulness of structures, forms, and routines. The people discussed in the cases are this chapters' co-authors.

CASE 1: ADOPTING: THE DANGER OF SCRIPTED MENTOR CURRICULA

One case study highlights the danger of forms overwhelming purposes. Judy's district had adopted a prepackaged program of guided events for mentors and new teachers to use together. Many district mentors had completed a 3-day training in use of materials focused on several teaching events. Events included maintaining classrooms, supporting all students' learning, and lesson planning. Materials came packaged and in a box for use by mentors. As one of the induction leaders, Judy found that new teachers reported little value in use of the materials, found the process swamped by too much paperwork, and hated "the dreaded box." Judy noted how, in some cases, mentors retreated to buddy roles, offering emotional support and sample lessons but little in the way of critical conversations about teaching and learning. In many cases, the box of materials had gone unopened. Why, Judy wondered, had mentors failed to adapt materials for use? After all, teachers wanted support for issues the events featured and reported appreciating being observed and reflecting with mentors.

Through inquiry, Judy learned that part of the problem was a failure in mentor development. In many cases, mentors were unclear about program goals and purposes and how program processes might link to improvement of practice. The district program had missed opportunities to adapt principles from the adopted packaged program to meet the needs of the individuals it served. Even more experienced mentors retreated to supplying lessons and other practical "goodies." Data showed that mentors could reply to survey questions in appropriate terminology but often did not understand reasons for program processes. Was this similar, Judy mused, to a teacher posting rules for classroom conduct versus student-generated rules that create student buy-in? In some cases, mentors had no prior knowledge of services they were expected to provide. Those who attended training sessions often received the same training over and over. Judy wondered about this. If educators need to differentiate lesson plans for different areas of student achievement, shouldn't mentor curriculum meet the needs of various levels of mentor knowledge and experience as well?

The California State Budget Act and Assembly Bill 2041 was passed to provide teacher induction successfully meeting beginning teachers' needs. Was that lost on some districts and teacher associations just concerned with fulfilling another state mandate? Soon, "judicious application of the paperwork" became the battle cry in Judy's district. Clearly, core principles had to be better translated to all parties. Professional development time was needed for mentors to more deeply understand program purposes, for pairs of mentors and teachers to adopt and adapt materials, and for mentors to collaborate with other mentors. Coordinators also needed to engage administrators so that they, too, were clear about program purposes and potential values.

CASE 2: ADOPTING AND ADAPTING WITH SCRIPTS AND BEYOND

Unlike Judy's group, Jennifer and Gordon used no packaged program but still adopted training and tools developed by external parties for their 1st year as induction coordinators. Regarding learning structures required to develop new knowledge, they knew adults were different from children, but what that meant for mentor curriculum was unclear. Like Judy, they found new mentors ready to provide emotional support but less ready to help new teachers question their practice and develop strategies to improve or refine it. They hoped the adopted tools would help. Mentors met 12 times over the year for full-morning or -afternoon workshops that included lecture, small- and large-group discussion, videos, and reflective writing related to effective mentoring strategies.

The team's research indicated that forms and models helped new coaches transition out of a "cheerleading" role and into one more substantive and educative. Bates's (2001) phases of a coaching conference and specific modeling of language provided new mentors with vocabulary and structure for reflective conversations with new teachers. Scripting what phases of a coaching conference sound like helped mentors facilitate meetings. In the area of reinforcement, as one example, Bates identified goals such as recommending to a new teacher continued use of a skill, explaining how such work promotes learning, and eliciting feedback about a teacher's perception of what has been discussed. Bates illustrated mentors' language with "sentence stems" such as "I saw you effectively use this strategy when you . . ." and "What do you think makes sense of what I just said about . . ." Mentors reported that the model allowed them to be more directive with new teachers as well as more supportive in acknowledging successes. One noted that it "gave me language I needed to do good observations." Another stated, "Now I can really engage my people in a way I couldn't before." The model also helped mentors make a subtle shift away from purely nurturing to guiding practice.

Tools from the New Teacher Center at the University of California, Santa Cruz also supported new mentors' data-gathering to guide new teachers' reflection. Most useful were tools for selective scripting (of a teacher's chosen focus of student and teacher comments in class); classroom maps to enable reflection on student performance; and student engagement tallies, often recorded on maps, to summarize lesson activity and student engagement trends. As a result of training and use of these instruments, 70% of the new coaches claimed they felt "Quite a bit" to "Very" effective in collecting observation data by the end of the year. However, mentors felt less comfortable using these data to guide support. Jennifer and Gordon learned that mentors needed structured time to role-play or practice reflective conferences based on data collected from classroom observation and needed guided practice in limiting data collection to specific areas outlined in a pre-observation conference. "I still overscript," one mentor admitted in a focus group, "because I'm afraid I'll leave out something important."

Jennifer and Gordon found it critical to scaffold instruction for new mentors with scripted training and tools, but mentors needed time to process information from seminars, to practice use of tools in groups, and to discuss difficult situations or cases. The program needed to be adapted for mentors to make sense of their new role and the knowledge needed to enact it well. Mentors repeatedly reported the need for time to brainstorm, to collaborate, to practice the language of coaching, to share and discuss issues, and to talk about real cases that might assist them in "owning" the role of coach.

One mentor struggled, for example, with how to get a new teacher to consider class and race when reviewing student achievement data. The mentor also had observed that the teacher's persistent classroom management issues centered on the only two African American students in class. When asked about these students, the teacher typically shifted responsibility from herself onto the students, noting, "I just think they would be more comfortable at another school," revealing an unwillingness to be more responsive. After explaining the case, the mentor role-played a 20-minute reflective conference with another mentor to assess the teacher's understanding of cultural differences and encourage her to consider how this understanding might affect her response to these students. Colleagues analyzed the conversation and offered suggestions. "[The conversation] not only allowed us to observe practice," one new mentor said, "but brainstorm possible solutions to an incredibly challenging situation."

Such comments encouraged the team to restructure seminars for the next year to allow more time to process, role-play, work with cases, and collectively problem-solve. Templates, structures, and protocols appeared helpful for new mentors' success, but the team's research strongly suggested it was essential to provide time at all sessions for mentors to process content, reflect on experiences, and internalize information through case study, role-play, and collective problem-solving. Expecting adults to just "get it" because they are adults and not students seemed reasonable in respecting an adult's wisdom, but the team found it was not what was needed for mentor growth. Scaffolding, templates, and chunking of material are congruent with adult learning theory. However, this case suggests that mentor development may benefit from both explicit scaffolding with tools adopted from external sources and reflective instructional time in which new processes are adapted to mentors' individual and group concerns. The case reminds us that mentor leaders face the same dilemma as the classroom teacher: needing to discern when to persist in content coverage and when to go deep in curriculum.

CASE 3: ADAPTING MENTOR CURRICULUM: FOREGROUNDING EQUITY IN A LARGE URBAN DISTRICT

Unlike Jennifer and Gordon, Susan K. and Virginia faced an urgent local need that incited them to focus and adapt their mentoring curriculum very specifically. Working with a large urban district serving mostly middle- to low-income youth of color, Susan, Virginia, and other district mentor leaders placed equity at the core of their induction program. Because of the inequitable educational status of African American and Latino students in the district and a low teacher retention rate, goals included supporting new teachers in culturally competent instruction and equity pedagogy to close the achievement gap and increase learning opportunities for targeted students of color. Though the district hired 400 new teachers per year, Susan and Virginia worked with a subset—26 new mentors and 26 new teachers. Approximately 50% of each group were teachers of color, and 43% of the new teachers were emergency-permit teachers. Core questions for the group's work were: What competencies must a mentor possess to effectively guide development of new teachers toward culturally responsive practices? What tools can help both new and experienced teachers reflect on and develop equity pedagogy?

The six California Standards for the Teaching Profession (CSTP) (CDE/ CCTC, 1996) provided a frame to guide teacher development, but they were inadequate to address needs of a district this size serving such a high percentage of traditionally underserved student populations. The CSTP broadstrokes "all" students without acknowledging specialized needs or inequities of the education system as it pertains to targeted students. This compelled the team to adapt the standards into a Culturally Responsive Standards for the Teaching Profession (CRSTP) framework. The tool is based on equity principles postulated by various researchers (Grossman, 1984; Kuykendall, 1992; Nieto, 1999; Nobles, 1991) who make explicit the requirement for teachers to know about their students' cultural and linguistic backgrounds. Modifications were made to give descriptions of practice greater cultural specificity and to make it easier for new teachers and mentors to use. The six CRSTP consist of descriptions of practice specially designed for teaching African American and Latino students, with performance scales to accompany each teaching standard and its various elements.

For example, the state standard of "Engaging and Supporting all Students in Learning" includes an element called "facilitating learning experiences that promote autonomy, interaction, and choice." The original document lists items that include "support and monitor student collaboration during learning activities." The CRSTP revised this to include "teacher facilitates learning experiences that promote divergent points of view." In so doing, the document signals an environment that is more than individuals working together, one that explicitly supports and even promotes perspectives that differ. The team also created two new items for this element: (1) "teacher works with families to extend students' learning and development of confidence and choice at home and school"; and (2) "teacher integrates multicultural and cross-cultural knowledge into curriculum." These items explicitly support linking school to family and to culturally diverse bodies of knowledge and experience.

From two-thirds to three-quarters of mentors rated their training in the CRSTP extensive, the quality high, and their ability to apply it high. One noted, "It is a great document. I'm very familiar with it and have been reading it like a 'bible.' And it really breaks it down, even though we are talking about helping beginning teachers here, even for veterans." A new teacher used the CRSTP framework as a self-assessment and reflective tool. She illustrated thoughtfully how she adapted culturally responsive practices based on cultural learning styles and student backgrounds in her teaching. She demonstrated how she continually revised a lesson plan she taught multiple times to adapt it to unique needs of each student and groups of students. She added scaffolding each time she taught the lesson to make it more accessible to diverse learners; made it more student-centered by encouraging students to be co-constructors of knowledge; and restructured learning experiences to help students develop metacognitive awareness. Like others, this teacher stated that she used the CRSTP to guide her assessment and modification of daily practice.

Data also revealed new teachers' receptivity to assistance in development of culturally responsive practices. Nearly three-fourths of new teachers indicated a high priority to have assistance with instructional planning to address specific needs of the focus populations, and 89% expressed as a high priority a desire to have effective culturally relevant literacy strategies shared with them. In addition, over 80% indicated willingness to open their classrooms for critique and specific feedback from mentors, while 60% wanted to invite mentors to come into their classrooms to demonstrate and model lessons. New teachers did not just want help with strategies for teaching "all" students, but overwhelmingly wanted assistance with developing culturally responsive practices for teaching underserved students.

Data indicated there was a group of mentors overall knowledgeable about equity work, confident about using culturally responsive pedagogy and instruments, and enthusiastic about advancing an equity agenda. The study also showed a group of new teachers eager to learn and to be supported in their development. The study was limited by self-reports, and no claim was made about closing the achievement gap. That work required future examination of how mentors directly "walk the equity talk" in work with new teachers, and how new teachers do so with students. It was critical at this level to ensure that support services and resources would be systematically and strategically placed to support and assess new teachers' application of equity pedagogy in the classroom.

Data also revealed several barriers that impeded the work. Over 50% of mentors, all full-time teachers, felt that their biggest challenge was finding time and developing structure to observe and meet with their new teachers; to collaborate with new teachers and other mentors; and to meet with other mentors to continue learning. Mentors wanted time to observe new teachers in the classroom; new teachers needed time to observe mentors in the classroom; mentors and teachers needed time to examine student work together and to engage in reflective conversation about what is observed and what is tried and where it all needs to go. Systemic barriers such as cumbersome hiring procedures and untimely, sometimes unresponsive bureaucratic practices impeded the work. The district's inability to recruit enough substitute teachers to provide release time for mentors and uncoordinated and unwieldy internal procedures prevented timely internal communication between administrative offices, and systemic flux in terms of personnel and structural changes had a negative impact on the work.

Nonetheless, despite these impediments, adaptation of state standards to focus mentors and new teachers on equity in classroom instruction provided focused instruction for the full team. Mentors recommended further refinement of pedagogical descriptors and a more condensed version of the adapted framework to achieve wider use of it as a self-assessment and self-reflective tool among new teachers and mentors. For Susan and Virginia, the core question remained: How do we build and sustain an individual and collective will to forge ahead in the work to close the achievement gap? Certainly institutional structures need to change, but careful attention to adaptation of tools to advance an equity agenda were key in teacher induction work in this project to help ensure that a focus remained on equitable learning opportunities for students too often underserved by schools.

CASE 4: INVENTING: A FOCUSED PROGRAM OF MENTORING FOR LITERACY

Unlike the other cases, this one highlights how induction leaders invented new mentoring curriculum based on needs assessments of students, teachers, mentors, and district. Suzi and Susan T. as new induction leaders held new responsibility for mentor development in the relatively small mentoring program in their mixed SES, fairly diverse suburban district. Capitalizing on the small size and on a districtwide literacy initiative, they focused mentor development sharply on subject matter knowledge and pedagogy, embedding the work in local concerns for grades K–6, and inventing support to advance a highly focused agenda. Their district stated a commitment to developing powerful, literate thinkers, one of their greatest challenges. New teachers reported insecurity about this charge. One new 1st-grade teacher noted, "When I first realized that helping a child develop into a lifelong reader was my responsibility . . . I was terribly overwhelmed. I wasn't sure that I could do it . . . I wasn't even sure where to start." Helping a child become a successful and lifelong reader is a daunting task for new teachers as they search for effective reading strategies. Mentor leaders Suzi and Susan asked: Would ongoing support directly impact new teachers' literacy practices and allow their students to consistently increase their reading levels? Their case illustrates inventing mentor development using original designs and local resources to meet district needs.

Just as new teachers needed knowledge and skills, so did their mentors. Professional development in reading strategies and student assessment were necessary. The team's use of district literacy coaches was extremely helpful. With that support, the team developed a variety of mentoring techniques, including demonstrations of ideas to engage students in literature activities and ideas for designing effective classroom centers. They created a library of professional development books on current research regarding literacy. The most powerful learning experiences for mentors resulted from weekly discussions about articles and findings read. These discussions often offered insights that could be shared with new teachers. Concurrent with this, mentors conducted informal observations of new teachers' reading programs early in the year to help design their mentoring program. They also surveyed new teachers on specific reading strategies to determine where to begin direct support. They learned that only one-third of new teachers used any kind of small-group or individualized instruction for literacy; only one-third used leveled books to guide reading instruction; and none taught reading for 100 minutes or more per week. Some teachers only occasionally used running records of literacy development and were then unclear as to their real purpose. A few teachers did not see their value at all. Teachers lacked background knowledge, appropriate resources, and confidence to approach instruction.

Mentors were buoyed by newfound confidence that research they had conducted could guide their mentoring agenda. They helped their new teachers take the assessment information they gathered and helped teachers design a program to take students to the next level of reading development. Assessment started to be looked upon as a "dipstick" to check student progress and assess student needs, and was used as a basis to design further instruction. Both mentors and new teachers learned some value of assessment. Mentor modeling of how to teach reading provided needed firsthand experience with what could be done and appeared to have a strong impact on new teachers' practices. Mentors taught guided reading groups for new teachers to observe, enabling teachers to see not only new ideas for teaching reading, but also classroom management techniques for maintaining student behavior of a large group while working with a small group. As teachers became more accomplished at applying newly learned reading strategies, they began small reading groups. Also, there now was more conversation about reading with students and less paperwork. Parents reported that their students were reading a lot more at home and became better at choosing books appropriate for their reading levels. Teachers themselves stated that they saw more growth in lower-achieving students' reading levels when compared with data from the prior year. In analyzing Benchmark Book assessments, the team documented progress with all students that year, some advancing well over the normal 1-year growth.

Students began reaping benefits. An end-of-year survey showed that two-thirds (or twice as many) new teachers now used small-group or individualized instruction for literacy. Seventy-five percent of the teachers taught reading 100 minutes or more per week, and 88% were now utilizing leveled books to drive instruction. The team felt confident that their focused induction program had a significant impact on the literacy programs of their new teachers. Their next important step was to document impact of that support on students beyond the pieces of achievement data and anecdotes they had collected. Success appeared attributable to the focused induction work, use of modeled strategies, videos of instructional approaches and other resources, conversations about literacy ideas, and the engagement of a district literacy coach. The mentor curriculum arose out of local need, responded explicitly to teachers' assessed needs in teaching literacy, and involved close tailoring through ongoing formative assessment of new teachers' literacy practices. To do the work, several mentors needed much of the same subject matter knowledge development that their mentees needed, and the mentor curriculum explicitly addressed this through material and human resources and ongoing reading and inquiry. The program was well resourced, with three full-time mentors/coordinators, and the entire project was supported by the leaders' own involvement in cycles of inquiry and involvement in the network of induction leaders.

INQUIRY AND MENTOR CURRICULUM IN CONTEXT

These cases teach us about the need to adopt and adapt and invent, the place for scripts and beyond, in designing mentor curriculum. Generic models of mentor curriculum provide templates and starting points, but when imported into local circumstances and reified as program, they likely will fall short. Research on teaching and standards for the profession repeatedly have advanced the tenet that good teaching is teaching in a context, with sensitivity to particular learners. The same tenet holds true for new teacher induction and mentor development.

The cases also remind us of the role of inquiry in enabling such understandings to emerge. Judy's inquiry enabled her to raise questions about the failure of her program to adopt and adapt. Surveys and coffee talks with mentors told Jennifer and Gordon of the power of scaffolds, but the emerging call for workshop time to engage tools more deeply and reflect on problematic cases helped these induction leaders develop a sense of balance for tools and process time based on group and individual need.

Susan K. and Virginia found through surveys, interviews, and observations that mentors and new teachers valued their adaptation of teaching standards to foreground equity. However, data also indicated that the tool needed further revision and that its value might depend also on engaging in district-level advocacy for structures to enable an equity agenda to remain in focus. Surveys and observations of new teachers helped Suzi and Susan T.'s team of mentors assess teacher needs in their project's focal area of developing literate thinkers. New student assessments as dipsticks and ongoing surveys of new teachers all served as formative assessments to help the mentor team learn about program needs and to respond in an ongoing fashion through curricular attention.

In all of these cases, then, induction leaders used data and deep reflection on their inquiry to gauge the kinds of supports needed in their particular and local curriculum of mentor development. Their particular insights help remind us that context matters, that mentor curriculum needs to engage adults as learners who benefit from tools and other scaffolds but whose particular understandings and attention to specific purposes and local needs call for ongoing attention to adaptation.

These are cases of new induction leaders working without road maps to design mentor curriculum. However, they tested new approaches and conducted inquiry in a network of equally engaged induction leaders. It is the accumulated knowledge of educators such as these that helps to highlight problems and successes in a new area of professional knowledge. The cases remind educators that investment in the learning of all youth requires investment in mentoring new teachers, which in turn requires investment of time and resources to develop quality induction programs in which mentor curriculum is carefully designed and monitored for effectiveness.

REFERENCES

Bates, M. (2001). *Professional development workshop for mentors.* Staff Development Institute, Inc., 10171 Kings Street, Los Alamitos, CA 90720.

California Department of Education/California Commission on Teacher Credentialing. (1996). *California standards for the teaching profession.* Sacramento: California Department of Education.

California State Budget Act and Assembly Bill 2041 (cpt 333–statutes of 1998). 1998–1999.

Gaston, E., Wilson, P., & Davis, C. (2001). *Support provider reflection: One step back, two steps forward.* The Mills PLuS BTSA Action Research Case Study. Leadership Network for Teacher Induction. Santa Cruz: University of California, Santa Cruz, The New Teacher Center.

Grossman, H. (1984). *Educating Hispanic students.* Springfield, IL: Charles C. Thomas.

Kuykendall, C. (1992). *From rage to hope: Strategies for reclaiming Black and Hispanic students.* Bloomington, IN: National Educational Service.

Nieto, S. (1999). *The light in their eyes.* New York: Teachers College Press.

Nobles, W. (1991). *African cultural educational praxis.* San Francisco: San Francisco State University Center for Applied Cultural Studies and Educational Achievement.

Wood, D., Bruner, J. S., & Ross, G. (1976). The role of tutoring in problem-solving. *Journal of Psychology and Psychiatry, 17,* 89–100.

CHAPTER 6

The Exploratorium Leadership Program in Science Education: Inquiry into Discipline-Specific Teacher Induction

Linda Shore and Laura Stokes

I took almost no science in college and then was asked to teach 7th- and 8th-grade science. I hated it! I knew nothing and didn't know who to ask for help. After all those years at the Exploratorium Teacher Institute, I became a real science teacher! I now love teaching science and my students voted my class as their favorite science class. This is a 180° turn of events.
— Teacher Institute Participant

Many teachers begin their careers inadequately prepared in subject matter and, as a result, need discipline-specific induction support. Even novices with strong content knowledge need to learn to successfully use materials and techniques particular to their subject areas to reach their student populations— developing pedagogical content knowledge situated in their own teaching contexts. How can beginning teachers gain the access to disciplinary knowledge and practical wisdom they need to build repertoires of best practice? A solution lies in knowledge and expertise held by effective veteran teachers. However, not every experienced teacher has the capacity to successfully apprentice a novice. How can veteran science teachers be selected, trained, and supported to use their knowledge to guide and support beginning teachers?

In this chapter we describe challenges faced and lessons learned from a content-specific teacher induction program developed by the San Francisco Exploratorium Teacher Institute (TI). We focus on the role of exemplary veteran science teachers who serve as program mentors and classroom coaches. The Exploratorium is a hands-on, interactive science museum whose mission is to foster deep understandings of scientific inquiry and transform science education in all places where science learning occurs: in schools, homes, and other museums. The Exploratorium TI has helped middle and high school science teachers bring authentic science inquiry into their classrooms for over 20 years. What distinguishes the TI from many professional development programs is that the support provided to science teachers is content-rich, coherent, and lifelong. With TI's new Teacher Induction Program—which includes a leadership training program for veteran science teachers who serve as mentors and coaches to new teachers—science teachers can be supported literally from induction through retirement.

THE CHALLENGE OF SUPPORTING NOVICE SCIENCE TEACHERS AND THEIR MENTORS

Science teachers face many challenges as they begin their careers. First, they typically are assigned to teach courses with content outside their subject areas of strength. As a result, novices need access to both content and pedagogical expertise. For example, a novice with a strong background in physics might be asked to teach biology and yet will almost certainly be isolated from other effective biology teachers and other sources of pedagogical content knowledge. Districts rarely provide release time or other supports that enable science teachers to mentor and support one another. In urban districts, the situation is made worse by the fact that there often are few veteran science teachers left in middle or high school departments, so there is little, if any, resident expertise. Second, novice science teachers need science-specific teaching materials, equipment, and resources required to infuse lessons with authentic science experiences. Many new science teachers lack the most basic supplies, such as glass beakers, balances for measuring mass, and sinks. Some classrooms even lack textbooks, especially in urban schools. Teachers in such circumstances need to develop skills to acquire critical resources. Finally, novice science teachers need models of good teaching practice. A traditional conception of science teaching as lecture springs from experiences new teachers have as students in undergraduate science courses where lectures predominate. Few novice science teachers ever have experienced authentic scientific inquiry as learners, and even fewer have had inquiry-based teaching modeled for them. Most teacher induction programs, while well-intentioned, do not have a strong subject-specific focus and do not match beginning teachers with mentor teachers who have the content knowledge and specific skills the novices are called upon to use. As a result, there is a limit to content-specific knowledge and skills that new teachers can gain through the mentoring process. In induction programs where mentors and novices teaching similar grades and subjects are matched, veteran teachers often do not receive the professional development and support needed to become successful mentors. Veteran science teachers, no matter how knowledgeable and talented, need education and support in learning to mentor. This chapter taps the Exploratorium's Teacher Induction Program as an example of an effort to foster discipline-specific induction and to support development of expert science teachers as mentors for such work.

SUPPORTING NEW SCIENCE TEACHERS
IN A SCIENCE-RICH COMMUNITY

With over 2,000 teacher alumni, each with a lifetime membership in the Exploratorium and its professional community of science teachers, the Teacher Institute (TI) revitalizes teachers and rekindles their love of science and science teaching. In 1998, as a response to the growing numbers of new science teachers struggling in local schools, and the opportunity presented by the fact that many of TI's most veteran alumni were searching for ways to pass on their accumulated wisdom and passion for teaching to future generations, the TI created the Teacher Induction Program. The program involves the most experienced TI alumni as mentors and classroom coaches of new teachers. These veterans embrace novice science teachers as members of the TI professional community, help introduce them to practices of teaching science as inquiry, and help induct them into the larger guild of the science teaching profession. As a 35-year veteran teacher who was a TI alumnus and program mentor noted, "I feel that at the end of one's career you give back to a profession that has given a lot to you."

Most new teachers in the TI program are employed by urban school districts serving disadvantaged students. Research on teacher retention demonstrates that in such urban school systems, over half of these novices leave the science teaching profession within the first 2 years due to a lack of support and teaching resources. This makes the Exploratorium's program particularly critical. One mentor noted, "I can't depend on my district for any resources."

The TI Induction Program is imbued with real science and the teaching of science. Hallmarks of its design are that TI alumni teachers (some retired or on sabbatical, some teaching full-time) serve as mentors and coaches of new teachers. Program activities relate directly to the context and teaching assignments of new teachers and occur within the Exploratorium's egalitarian and nonevaluative culture of learning. The working hypothesis that gives shape to the program is this: a discipline-specific beginning teacher program that links novices with scientists and with experienced, exemplary teachers who themselves are part of a professional community of learners will produce more effective science teaching practices earlier in a new teacher's career. The 2-year induction program for new science teachers includes in-class coaching, science content workshops, pedagogy workshops, and support group meetings during the year. Novices also are required to attend a 4-week summer institute that involves working with Exploratorium scientists on science and inquiry and working with veteran teachers on development of science lessons and units. From 1998 to 2003, the induction program has served nearly 250 novice science teachers from San Francisco, San Mateo County, and other districts in the Bay Area. Of those, about 90% have graduated from the 2-year program, are still teaching science, and are TI alumni with lifetime access to Exploratorium resources and programs.

Benefits accrue when veteran teachers mentor novices, but there are challenges. First, a program needs real, productive opportunities for veterans to draw upon their knowledge as they work with novices. In a science-specific program, activities must be designed so that veterans with specific backgrounds work in customized ways with novices who have specific learning needs and teaching assignments. A veteran chemistry teacher supporting a novice chemistry teacher likely will need to discuss ways to introduce potentially toxic or explosive substances to students. This issue is less likely to arise for a new astronomy teacher. Second, novices need both knowledge application and opportunities to reflect on practice, so the induction program needs subject-specific activities that provide both experiences. A novice might attend a workshop on magnetism with inquiry-based experiences or a lesson-planning workshop to learn how to best sequence activities to promote student learning. But eventually the novice needs in-class support to sequence earth science lessons about the earth's magnetic field and opportunities to reflect on this practice. Third, the program needs to provide sufficient training and support to veterans in their work as mentors.

"Teaching Boxes" as a Vehicle for Science-Specific Mentoring

In the Exploratorium's induction program, activities bring together veteran science teachers and novices. These include classroom coaching, content and pedagogy workshops, support groups, and summer institutes. Within these are generative structures designed to develop novices' teaching abilities and to tap veterans' leadership capacities. One of these, construction of "Teaching Boxes," helps veterans make underlying knowledge explicit while helping novices gain teaching skills and critically needed materials. Novices participate in the 4-week Introductory Summer Institute featuring the learning of science through inquiry. Facilitated by staff scientists and educators, novices interact with Exploratorium exhibits designed to ignite curiosity and raise questions about the natural world. In the museum classrooms, teachers engage in inquiry experiences that foster deeper understandings of science content and process.

At the same time, veteran teachers participate in the Leadership Institute, a core component of the Leadership Program. For 6 hours each week, novices and mentors work collaboratively on construction of Teaching Boxes. This activity was invented in response to a challenge faced early in the Induction Program when a serious conflict arose between novices' immediate need to have "stuff" for their classrooms and mentors' desire to share a lifetime of ideas about teaching and learning. Because novices were focused on day-to-day survival in classrooms with few supplies or resources, they wanted mentors to supply them with materials and lessons they could use immediately. They were not particularly interested in (or ready for) deep discussions about teaching and learning. Mentors, who were intensely reflecting upon their classroom experiences and pedagogical philosophies with peers in the Leadership Institute, felt a strong need to pass on experiences and knowledge to the next generation of science teachers. They were not at all interested in merely delivering science materials, lessons, and units to novices devoid of the deep thinking and care that had gone into their development over the years.

TI staff, sympathetic to both perspectives, wanted to foster in-depth and meaningful dialogues between novices and veterans, but in the context of the science content the novices were actually going to be teaching. To accomplish this, staff developed a "product" that novices and veterans create together called the Teaching Box. Not only would building such a box together provide the "stuff" the novices hungered for, but it also would give veteran teachers occasion to externalize their internalized wisdom about pedagogy, learning, and assessment. Moreover, these deeper conversations would be more meaningful to novices because they would be centered on a unit the novices would actually teach.

The Teaching Box is analogous to products used to develop knowledge and skills in other apprenticeship learning environments (Collins, Brown, & Newman, 1989). Apprentice tailors start by working on a simple project, like the straight seam of a pair of pants. The master tailor directs and offers skill and practical wisdom developed over a lifetime, until the novice achieves a level of mastery to move on to another, more complex project. In the Induction Program, the first task is to learn to develop a coherent science lesson to help students build conceptual understanding. Building that lesson involves gathering materials and resources for the hands-on component and designing how to use them in the lesson. From there, novices add new science teaching skills to their repertoires, such as development of authentic student assessment tools or the ability to sequence lessons into coherent units. Novices take the boxes with them to use in teaching; copies also are put into the Exploratorium's teacher resource library so all teachers have access to them. In the spirit of the Exploratorium's approach, mentors continually help novices design materials and activities that use hands-on experience to provoke student inquiry and help them develop science concepts. Further, veteran teachers help novices link teaching to state standards through creation of teaching boxes that address core science topics, for example "Measurement," "What Is Science?" "The Cell," and "Earthquakes."

One mentor referred to co-constructing the box as a "focal point . . . to share my story with the novices and to convey ideas." Another stated about a new teacher that the main benefit was

> sitting and talking about what he had done before with the subject and what was unsatisfactory about it and then talking about what we could do to make it more successful. . . . So we scaled back on how many topics he was trying to cover and decided to go into more depth. He had a lot of involvement in planning the box. I think that was the point of doing the boxes, not to have one product, but to have gone through the process of thinking through a unit and deciding how to make it feel better next time he taught it and take the model and that experience and use it in his other subjects. It was sort of like an ongoing work in process; he could refine it and add to it and change it as he taught it and got feedback.

A new teacher remarked:

> What has been opened to me is the wealth of resources that I didn't know about before. It is more than building a curriculum box—it is the process of the curriculum box. I started to see the linearity of planning a lesson—how to go from A to B. We started with the end result, which was to teach the concept of density, and by extension, I now have developed a curriculum that starts with linear measurement and works all the way through.

While mastery of the art of science teaching takes a lifetime, the Teaching Box experience is an important early step in the journey.

Constructing a Genetics Teaching Box

One group of new teachers and veterans created a genetics teaching box. One lesson was about DNA, borrowed from an experienced biology teacher and Exploratorium faculty member who had developed it for her class after interacting with a DNA exhibit at the Exploratorium. At the heart of the lesson was students' construction of a model of DNA that they used to understand the structure and function of DNA. The veteran teacher had used the model many times; key to its success was that as students put it together, the correct structure of DNA emerged and appeared to them. This enabled them to develop their own understanding, through firsthand observation, that the two types of base pairs (cytosine and guanine, and adenine and thymine) always go together, and how those base pairs attach to the sugar-phosphate sequences that constitute the "railings" of the DNA ladder. The teacher not only knew the DNA structure herself but knew how to create a model and process of construction that would serve the core scientific process and purpose of enabling students to see and study something very small by making a model. She also had taught this lesson and could tell novices how long to give students to make the model and other management issues specific to the lesson.

Students then string together their models to make one large model, enabling the teacher to demonstrate ways in which sequences of many base pairs occur on strands of DNA. The teacher then could take new teachers through a number of lessons from this model—for example, about how some alterations in some base pairs create mutations with serious consequences and others that are harmless. Having taught this lesson before, the teacher could identify for new teachers the kinds of concepts that can be taught with this model, what students are likely to ask or be confused about, how and when to integrate material from a textbook, and so on.

Because the group working on the genetics box included both middle and high school life science teachers (several novices, three veterans), discussion turned to ways to adapt or extend the lesson for varied grade levels. They talked about how to introduce the relationship between DNA and RNA, and at what level of depth to study the role of RNA in protein synthesis. The teacher who had originated the lesson shared experiences with different levels of students, and the other veteran biology teachers also were able to share ideas about how to extend the lesson for higher-level students, link it with other biology concepts, shrink it to fit a shortened school period, and in other ways situate the lesson in varied contexts. The discussion enabled the novices to hear experienced teachers' judgments about core science concepts that are especially important and about realities of teaching science in ever-changing contexts. It also gave the novices a chance to contribute ideas for teaching DNA and for adapting the lesson to their own curriculum, with veterans who could give feedback and build on their ideas. The novices could not only compile specific knowledge from veterans but could also troubleshoot and research teaching ideas in a safe group of colleagues, rather than risking trial and error in the classroom.

Joint construction of the box—with new teachers making the model and seeing how to learn from it, deconstructing the lesson, discussing both content within it and particularities of teaching—all of this was possible because of three kinds of critical knowledge the veterans had: (1) knowledge of DNA, RNA, and their role in life; (2) knowledge of how to teach biology in real school conditions to different levels of students; and (3) knowledge of how to use these specific teaching materials for optimal learning of a specific lesson. This is just one of dozens of experiences new teachers in this program have, in workshops at the Exploratorium and at their schools when coaches observe their teaching or model lessons for them. It is within this science-rich community of practice that new science teachers can gain confidence and a foundational repertoire of tools.

Exploratorium Leadership Program

Since 1998, 50 veteran Exploratorium teachers have completed a 2-year program of learning to mentor new science teachers.

Selection of mentors. The program staff developed selection criteria for mentors and coaches consistent with induction program goals, so veteran teachers could bring a strong foundation of appropriate knowledge and skill to their work with new science teachers. The novice program aims to induct teachers into a vision of best practices that includes inquiry, authentic science, and strong science content. Therefore, veterans selected as mentors and coaches need exceptional skills from the start. Through applications, interviews, and classroom observations, staff consider several questions:

- Are applicants reflective about their own science teaching practices?
- Are they able to clearly articulate rationales for the teaching choices they make?
- Do their lessons and units include opportunities for students to do authentic science?
- Are Exploratorium activities and materials used in lessons?
- Do applicants possess strong science content knowledge?
- Are they willing to articulate and share expertise with novices?

Mentors and coaches must be able to make pedagogical knowledge explicit, have experience in curriculum design and unit planning, possess strong science content knowledge, have leadership experience or potential, and demonstrate a clear commitment to inquiry-based teaching and learning.

Defining roles and generative structures. The Exploratorium's Induction Program has two broad goals for new teachers. One is to induct them into the Exploratorium TI community so they can regard the Exploratorium as their professional home for the rest of their careers. The second is to offer them experiences and tools that will, in the formative classroom years, start them on a path of development as effective teachers of authentic science. Program roles defined for veteran teachers and activities they engage in with novices are designed to maximize what veteran teachers can contribute to new teachers' development.

Veteran teachers in the program-defined role of "mentors" (who are usually full-time teachers) are primarily responsible for inducting novices into the culture and traditions of the TI and directing novices to appropriate Exploratorium teaching resources. Mentors also lead after-school and Saturday novice workshops on common teaching challenges (e.g. classroom management, discipline, and parental involvement), but in the context of inquiry-based science teaching. A workshop on "Parental Involvement" might include an introduction to science activities that involve families; a workshop on "Classroom Management" might include strategies for distributing science materials—which can be sharp, toxic, breakable, alive, and/or otherwise vulnerable to mishandling—in ways that are safe and respectful and retain students' attention.

Veteran teachers in the role of "coaches" (retired teachers or teachers on sabbatical) are primarily responsible for inducting novices into a larger guild of the science teaching profession. They help novices develop strategies of effective inquiry-based teaching and learning. Their primary role is to model science lessons for novices in the novices' classrooms, provide one-on-one support as novices try inquiry-based lessons with students, and help novices reflect on their practice with the goal of improving their pedagogical content knowledge. Coaches also help novices in other ways at school sites. For example, they help novices become less isolated by helping them build relationships with other science teachers in their schools and with their principals. Coaches also help orient novices to educational resources available in the school and district, sometimes literally helping them to find storage closets and to identify and learn to use science equipment buried inside. In either role, coaches and mentors are assigned to novices so that the content knowledge and experience of the veteran teacher are as closely matched as possible to the teaching assignment and knowledge needs of the novices. While the coach/mentor roles are somewhat distinct in the TI program, there is considerable crossover between them.

Training and supporting coaches and mentors. The analogy between supporting mentor teachers and preparing new teachers cannot be overstated. New science teachers start careers with little or no direct experience with student-centered, inquiry-based teaching and learning. Similarly, master teachers start their new roles having rarely if ever experienced being mentored or witnessing successful mentoring. New science teachers typically try out new pedagogical strategies in isolation, without benefit of the help of an experienced master teacher. Likewise, many mentors work with novices without benefits of formal practice sessions, coaching, or reflection. Allowing mentors to sink or swim in their new roles can be as damaging as it is for novice science teachers.

Even with careful selection of veteran teachers who bring the right combination of knowledge and skills, the Exploratorium staff has learned that training of mentor and coaches must include the following:

1. Veteran teachers need to observe and experience models of exemplary mentoring in support groups and through in-class coaching.
2. During these observations, the critical features of successful mentor support and classroom coaching must be made explicit.
3. Veteran teachers need opportunities to practice their new skills, preferably in a safe environment where the risks of failure are minimized.
4. Veteran teachers need opportunities to reflect on the development of their new skills, preferably with the input of master teachers who are highly skilled at working with beginning teachers.

Summer Leadership Institute participants are required to work with novices for 6 hours each week on the teaching boxes. This work is carefully guided and monitored by program staff so that veterans, while sharing knowledge with novices, also are becoming more perceptive and skilled in interactions with novices. Participants also engage in moderated group discussions and activities that develop and refine their abilities to:

- Reflect, critique, model, and coach.
- Plan workshops on topics helpful to new teachers, such as science materials management, student discipline, and organizational survival skills.
- Identify and locate science lessons, curriculum materials, resource agencies, science organizations, and other key resources that might be helpful to novices.

- Develop "starting points" to initiate relationships and diagnose the learning needs of the beginning teachers.

The skill of initiating relationships and diagnosing the needs of novice teachers is a critically important component of the preparation of mentors and coaches because of the customized nature of the program. While novices are required to participate in workshops, summer institutes, and support group meetings, they are provided with an extensive menu of options so the program can be tailored to meet specific needs. It is the veteran teachers' primary responsibility—guided by staff—to identify what type of support and coaching each novice needs. In assisting novices, veterans take into consideration their content background, specific teaching assignments, and comfort level with hands-on teaching. During the school year, as the mentoring and coaching work unfolds, TI staff stay in contact with the veteran teachers individually to help them plan specific activities and to problem-solve. Twice per year, the mentors and coaches gather together and reflect collectively on their work.

Mentors and coaches are required to complete the summer Leadership Institute prior to beginning a 2-year commitment to work with novices. At the end of the first year, those identified as particularly successful are strongly encouraged to participate in the Leadership Institute the following year as well, to bring the voice of experience to training new veterans. They share successful coaching and mentoring strategies developed in the field and provide critical insights into challenges faced by novices in their teaching contexts. These experienced leaders also are critical in helping novices assemble Teaching Boxes, while concurrently modeling mentoring strategies for new leaders in the program.

TRADE-OFFS AND LESSONS LEARNED

The Exploratorium's Induction and Leadership programs may be unique, but they can be re-created or adapted in other contexts. Doing so requires understanding the considerable strengths and attributes of the program and its work, but also—as with any model—understanding inherent trade-offs of the program's approach. For example, designing a menu-driven induction program that taps the best of what individual veteran teachers know and can do is probably inconsistent with programs that must provide standardized experiences. A menu-driven induction program may be practically impossible to implement in large-scale education systems (such as school districts) where state and/or national policy mandates drive decisions about induction goals. In fact, the menu approach so critical to the Exploratorium's success may only work in institutions like the Teacher Institute that exist outside (but in close relationship to) the formal system. TI's teacher members have the intellectual autonomy and will to focus primarily on their individual teaching and learning and secondarily on policy mandates.

Second, by aiming to serve varied needs of new science teachers, the Exploratorium program requires veterans to use a great deal of discretion and judgment in creating relationships with novices. Veterans help novices identify what they need, and then the veterans are responsible for selecting and providing novices with specific support indicated. In one case, a novice might be struggling because of a lack of physics content knowledge. In another, a novice's students may be having trouble learning because there is a problem with classroom discipline. The Exploratorium model really takes an "expert consultant" approach, within its flexible framework of program options. This places considerable demands on the wisdom and skill of each veteran teacher. There have been times when participants (and thus the program staff) have struggled to learn what the TI calls "novice teacher triage" —the art of identifying what "ails" a novice, prescribing an appropriate "treatment," and conducting follow-up "checkups." The lesson learned here, again, is that heavy investment is needed in selection, training, and support of veterans working with new teachers.

REVITALIZING THE PROFESSION THROUGH SUPPORT OF SCIENCE-SPECIFIC MENTORS

Support programs for new teachers typically socialize them into organizational cultures of school and general norms of teaching. Induction programs rarely introduce teachers to a lasting, well-supported professional community knit together by abiding interests in learning more about, and teaching, a subject discipline. One hallmark of all Exploratorium programs for teachers is that they reflect and exemplify the true nature of the disciplines—the excitement, rigor, and conceptual depth of learning in science. The Exploratorium teacher network spans school and district boundaries and is informed and inspired by a rich vision of science and of science teaching. The literature on teacher professional development points to subject-specific networks as playing a vital role in teacher learning and renewal. In fact, an important lesson that can be learned from this program is about the value of linking two goals—to support teachers in developing specific skills of science teaching, and to revitalize the profession by enabling caring, skillful veterans to embrace new teachers as colleagues and members of a dynamic community of science teachers.

To accomplish both goals requires a substantial investment in design of programs and activities in which experienced veteran teachers can draw upon their own pedagogical content knowledge in the support of new teachers' development. The Exploratorium has made this investment in two ways. First, it has supported a professional community of science teachers for two decades—nurturing their love of science, enhancing their knowledge of science, and supporting their development as effective teachers of science. For hundreds of TI alumni, the Exploratorium represents an intellectual lifeline, an antidote to sometimes grinding conditions of schools that can cause burnout. It also represents a career-long training ground. In effect, the Exploratorium has been preparing veteran teachers as potential mentors for the entire tenure of those teachers' membership in the Exploratorium community. Carefully selected veterans thus bring to the program the critical knowledge base—as well as Exploratorium-nourished beliefs and values—about science and about the teaching of science. Additionally, they bring years of experience amid schooling conditions that make such teaching approaches ever more challenging. What the Leadership Program adds to this considerable (but latent) capacity for mentoring is an opportunity in the form of structured interactions with novice teachers that enable veterans to share their wisdom and support with other new mentors developing these new skills.

NOTES

The Teacher Institute is directed by Linda Shore, supported by Victoria Brady, Paul Doherty, Karen Kalumuck, Lori Lambertson, Eric Muller, Don Rathjen, Anna Rochester, Modesto Tamez, and Blake Wigdahl. Laura Stokes has conducted evaluation research on the Beginning Teacher Program, along with colleagues from Inverness Research Associates, including Mark St. John (President), Judy Hirabayashi, Samantha Broun, and Dianne Maxon.

The Exploratorium Teacher Induction Program is funded by the National Science Foundation, the Noyce Foundation, the Carnegie Corporation of New York, the Joseph P. Heller Foundation, the Crocker Foundation, the Walter and Elyse Haas Foundation, and the RGK Foundation. Opinions stated herein are those of the authors and do not reflect opinions of these funders.

REFERENCE

Collins, A., Brown, J. S., & Newman, S. E. (1989). Cognitive apprenticeship: Teaching the crafts of reading, writing, and mathematics. In L. B. Resnick (Ed.), *Knowing, learning, and instruction: Essays in honor of Robert Glaser* (pp. 453–494). Hillsdale, NJ: Erlbaum.

CHAPTER 7

Curriculum to Support Mentor Development: Lessons from Field-Tested Practices

Barbara Davis

In many new teacher support programs, mentors are left to work with new teachers with little guidance. The Santa Cruz New Teacher Project, however, has developed and tested tools and strategies to support learning how to mentor new teachers. This chapter samples those used successfully and disseminated throughout the United States by the New Teacher Center at the University of California, Santa Cruz. A Curriculum of Professional Development for Mentors illustrates the scope and sequence of mentor development, with tools embedded. A Repertoire of Interactive Approaches offers ways to organize and guide a mentor's selection of tools and strategies tailored to an individual new teacher, in a particular time and circumstance. Three tools illustrate how mentors can move new teachers' practice forward: Mentoring Conversation Protocol, Collaborative Assessment Log, and Analysis of Student Work. The chapter includes lessons learned from using these tools, challenges and cautions, and opportunities mentors have to strengthen the profession.

CURRICULUM OF PROFESSIONAL DEVELOPMENT FOR MENTORS

What sort of mentors do we want to develop? What are the essential understandings and skills that would best support mentors in their work?

How can we support their leadership, vision, and passion? How can we develop mentors with knowledge, will, and power to challenge the status quo? These questions help shape the curriculum of mentor professional development.

Figure 7.1 shows a sample curriculum that, like others, gained power because it was developed collaboratively, in response to local needs and context. Three circled items in the figure are tools introduced later in this chapter.

The figure shows four focus areas of the curriculum run over the course of a year, presented here in two-month time blocks. The first area is the Formative Assessment System (FAS), tools the mentor uses to engage new teachers in examination of classroom practice. Central is the goal-setting process where novices assess their own teaching practice, with the guidance of their mentor, on a Continuum of Teacher Development and then summarize strengths and areas of challenge. Together the mentor and the teacher determine a goal for improvement and develop a professional growth plan. The plan is revised over the course of the year. Also critical to the process is the inquiry cycle, begun in the "Oct./Nov." column. The mentor supports the novice, using new knowledge of students and community as they focus on analyzing student work and planning lessons based on differentiated instructional techniques.

Figure 7.1 also shows the second focus area, the Formative Assessment System Support Strategies. In addition to tools, there are a number of skills, techniques, and strategies a mentor needs to know and use to engage the new teacher in this work so that it is meaningful, impacts students, and provides insight into growth as a colleague and member of the school community. For example, the Collaborative Assessment Log (circled item in Row 1 of the figure) is a tool used to record interaction between a mentor and novice. However, a strategy that is critical to successful use of this tool is Holding a Mentoring Conversation (Figure 7.1, Row 2), where the mentor skillfully engages in active listening and the language of coaching.

Analysis of Beginning Teacher Development is the third focal area. This is where, in a facilitated collaborative group, mentors share documentation of their work with new teachers and analyze a teacher's performance based on professional teaching standards (italicized in Row 3). Mentors problem-solve real issues and gain insights and direction for next steps. This is also where mentors can increase their own knowledge and understanding of teaching standards. The fourth area is the Mentor Formative Assessment. Mentors form coaching partnerships, select a new teacher for ongoing case study analysis, set their own professional goals for mentoring, periodically review progress toward those goals, and reflect on their growth—both successes and challenges.

We have found that mentors need a collaborative learning environment to develop their knowledge and skills. Weekly mentor meetings are the con-

Figure 7.1. A Curriculum of Professional Development for Mentors

Focus	Aug./Sept.	Oct./Nov.	Dec./Jan.	Feb./Mar.	Apr./May
Formative Assessment System (FAS)	• Using the Collaborative Assessment Log • Exploring School and Community Resources • Setting Professional Goals	• Assembling a Class Profile • 1st Inquiry Cycle (Analyzing Student Work, Planning Lessons, Communicating with Parents)	• Conducting Observations • Reviewing Progress at Midyear	• 2nd Inquiry Cycle (Analyzing Student Work, Planning Lessons, Communicating with Parents) • Conducting Observations	• Reflecting on Professional Growth • Sharing Promising Practices: A Colloquium
FAS Support Strategies	• Using the Interactive Journal • Holding a Mentoring Conversation • Communicating with Site Administrators • Linking FAS with Content Standards	• Organizing and Keeping Records • Observing for Teaching Standards • Problem-Solving • Building Partnerships with Principals • Teaching Special Populations	• Building Partnerships with Principals • Practicing, Problem-Solving, and Calibrating the Use of FAS Tools • Mentoring for Equity	• Building Partnerships with Principals • Observing Veteran Teachers	• Reflecting and Providing Feedback • Organizational Support and Systems
Analysis of Beginning Teacher Development	• Analyzing Beginning Teacher Development: *Effective Environment*	• Analyzing Beginning Teacher Development: *Assessing Student Learning and Planning Instruction*	• Reflecting on Case Study	• Analyzing Beginning Teacher Development: *Subject Matter Knowledge and Engaging All Students*	• Reflecting on Case Study • Sharing Promising Practices
Mentor Formative Assessment	• Self-Assessing on Mentor Continuum • Setting Mentor Professional Goals • Selecting a Beginning Teacher Case Study • Analyzing Beginning Teacher Development: *Effective Environment* • Establishing Coaching Partners	• Reviewing FAS Documents of Case Study • Analyzing Beginning Teacher Development: *Assessing Student Learning and Planning Instruction* • Conducting In-Field Observations and Reflecting Conferences with Coaching Partners	• Reviewing Progress Toward Goals • Reviewing Progress of Case Study • Reviewing Results of Induction Survey	• Reviewing FAS Documents of Case Study • Conducting In-Field Observations and Reflecting Conferences with Coaching Partners • Analyzing Beginning Teacher Development: *Subject Matter Knowledge and Engaging All Students*	• Reflecting on Mentor Professional Growth • Reviewing Progress of Case Study about Beginning Teacher

text where the mentoring curriculum that sustains the quality of our program and helps develop high-quality mentors is implemented.

An example of a meeting agenda (Figure 7.2) highlights how learning time supports mentors in developing and refining skills, understanding concepts, applying knowledge and skills, reflecting upon practice, and planning next steps. Reviewing business and logistics aids communication flow among mentors. The Closing is short but critical for debriefing the meeting process and determining future focus. Beyond a curriculum of mentor development, we have found that a mentor needs a framework to organize and guide use

Figure 7.2. Mentor Professional Development Meeting Agenda

Connecting	
1:00–1:30	**Analysis of an Assessment Success:** Personal reflection. Partner share. *Purpose:* generate criteria for assessments that measure essential learning and provide information that informs instruction
1:45–1:55	Review Agenda and Minutes: Select Recorder_____
Learning	
1:55–2:10	**Learning 1: Case Study of Assessment:** Table groups. Discussion, strategizing. *Purpose:* examine dilemmas of assessment related to classroom instruction and issues of equity
2:10–2:20	Break
2:20–2:45	**Learning 2: Coaching Skills:** Role-play. *Purpose:* practice work as mentors and receive feedback to improve coaching skills
2:45 - 3:05	**Learning 3: Mentor Collaborative Log:** Reflective write. Triad conversation. *Purpose:* reflect on personal strengths and challenges regarding assessment and mentoring work
Managing	
3:05–3:15	**Business and Announcements** • New Teacher Symposium, Feb. 2–4 • County Office Workshop on Differentiated Instruction, March 21 • Bring to next meeting: completed case study, Analysis of Student Work • Next Meeting Date: January 6
Closing	
3:15–3:30	**Reflections and Next Steps:** Process debrief. *Purpose:* record on a public chart participant reflections on meeting process and content. What worked? What needs changing? What questions or next steps?

of various tools and strategies to tailor support to meet the individual developmental needs of new teachers.

A REPERTOIRE OF INTERACTIVE APPROACHES

What is the array of interactive approaches a mentor needs for work with new teachers? Under what circumstances would a mentor use a particular approach? How can mentors tailor conversations and behaviors to match the needs of each new teacher? It is critical that mentors learn to identify clues, cues, and circumstances—the language and behaviors—that can inform their selection of appropriate approaches and tools. They learn to "read" the mentoring situation (Orland, 2001). Following Glickman (2002) on instructional leadership approaches in work with teachers, Figure 7.3 shows how a mentor can consider approaches to employ in conversations with novices. In the instructive approach, choices are offered but are more limited, focused, and possibly attached to expectations and time lines. The collaborative approach is characterized by collegial reflection, problem-solving, and inquiry, each participant contributing ideas and resources. In the facilitative approach, power shifts to the new teacher, and the mentor is an active prober, using language of listening, paraphrasing, and clarifying.

Figure 7.3. A Repertoire of Interactive Approaches between Mentor and Beginning Teacher

Instructive	*Collaborative*	*Facilitative*
• mentor controls interaction • information flows from mentor to new teacher • locus of control is external—resides with mentor or other influencing factors outside of the new teacher • mentor offers suggestions and solutions	• mentor guides interaction without controlling it • mentor and new teacher co-construct solutions and materials	• new teacher actively directs flow of information • mentor facilitates new teacher's thinking and problem-solving • new teacher self-assesses and self-prescribes • locus of control resides in new teacher

Adapted from Glickman (2002)

The new teacher clearly has the lead in moving toward his or her own sense of efficacy and professional autonomy.

While mentors may use all three approaches, the right-pointing arrow shows how we have found success when the locus of control in mentoring moves toward greater teacher autonomy. In most mentor-and-new-teacher interactions, we have found the entry point usually in the collaborative range, where a professional relationship is acknowledged and the new teacher's receptiveness may be increased. We also have found that effective mentors may shift approaches, within a matter of minutes during a conversation, to meet a novice's needs. Working with mentors in professional development activities such as case study analysis, video observation, problem-posing/problem-solving, and role-playing can strengthen a mentor's ability to select the appropriate approach to best meet the needs of each new teacher, at a particular time and in specific circumstances. As mentors become more skillful in determining which strategic approach to take in a given situation, they can reach into their tool kit and frame the work to connect with novices where they are and then take those steps to move them forward. The next sections review three tools we have found critical to professional development of new teachers.

THREE MENTORING TOOLS

Tool 1: Mentoring Conversation Protocol

The tool and its uses. In professional development, mentors in our program observe and practice, through video or role-play, the language and behaviors of a conversation that moves a teacher's practice forward. Mentors learn and practice language of support. This includes paraphrasing (What I'm hearing then is . . . , In other words . . .) and clarifying (Let me see if I understand . . . , Tell me a little more about . . .); and asking mediational questions to promote analysis of what worked or didn't or to hypothesize about what might happen (What would it look like if . . . ? What sort of impact do you think . . . ?). Other forms of supportive language include seizing the teachable moment, a spontaneous opportunity to fill in an instructional gap and/or take the new teacher to the next level of practice; offering suggestions (Some things to keep in mind when dealing with . . . , Something you might consider trying is . . . , There are a number of approaches . . .); and generally responding in reflective, invitational, and nonjudgmental ways.

A Mentoring Conversation Protocol supports mentors in developing skills of using this type of conversation. Four areas are addressed:

1. *Assess the beginning teacher's needs* by making connections and building trust, and identifying successes and challenges.
2. *Establish a focus for work* by paraphrasing and clarifying.
3. *Support the teacher's movement forward* by direct teaching, collaborative problem-solving/work, and reflective questioning.
4. *Promote accountability* by identifying specific next steps and agreeing to follow up.

When learning to use this tool, mentors are reminded of the continual need to establish and maintain a trusting relationship with the new teacher; to honor and acknowledge attributes the teacher brings to the profession; and to truly believe the teacher wants to succeed, wants students to learn, and is capable of making decisions and solving problems. This tool can be used in a formal structured scheduled meeting, or it can guide a quick conversation as follow-up to another activity or event. It can be used by the mentor in a sequential and deliberate manner, or it can guide conversation when the mentor meanders, following the natural course of the conversation, but with the intent that all components are covered.

Many mentors are comfortable in acquiring and understanding information and using it in a concrete, logical manner, that is, knowing the tools and structures used to carry out mentoring responsibilities and having a clear understanding about various approaches to employ when interacting with a new teacher. Being a mentor can be taught relatively successfully through professional development embedded within a comprehensive induction system. However, mentoring also involves attributes such as instinct, reflectivity, creativity, and problem-solving. The mentor needs to *be* mentored/coached/ taught in ways that support these attributes. This might involve discussion with colleagues, analysis of their own practice, setting goals, thinking conceptually about the role of mentor, and engaging in risk-taking actions.

Lessons learned from using the tool. In their conversations with novices, we have more often than not seen new mentors tend to avoid directive approaches in efforts to maintain relationship. Mentors with advanced experience and training operate more skillfully among various approaches. In the early years of our work, we realized we had overemphasized a need for relationship building and coaching language. We noted that mentors entered this new role with little understanding of adult learning and engaged with novices as if they were students. We, therefore, felt it imperative to counterbalance this need to "teach" and "direct" by focusing on more facilitative aspects of the role. We began to realize we were off-track when our mentors finally said, in desperation, *Can't we just tell them what to do sometimes?*

We urge program leaders to find that balance when designing professional development for mentors.

We also learned that new mentors tend to stay in a more prescriptive comfort zone when holding a conversation. It is easier to stick to the protocol closely—in sequence, as well as content—and not let the conversation flow naturally. Paraphrasing and clarifying questions are used most often by new or less skillful mentors. They seem less inclined to move to a more collaborative or instructive stance such as asking mediational questions, problem-solving, giving suggestions, or taking advantage of teachable moments. They tend not to actually get to the place where their new teachers are visibly moving ahead. They don't quite get to a point of "pushing" their novices. Our interpretation is that mentors may equate becoming more directive or instructive with being authoritative. Mentors face tensions when they try to become more directive, as it challenges their norms of relationship-building. However, educative mentoring responds to the here-and-now concerns and emotional needs of novices and creates learning opportunities that move new teachers' practice forward (Feiman-Nemser, 2001).

We also learned that some new mentors may go overboard with a directive approach, challenging new teachers' autonomy. This is particularly evident when novices enter the profession with little preparation; have been assigned more difficult or inappropriate placements; and/or are working in "toxic" professional school cultures. In a desperate attempt to fix it or because they themselves operate in nonsupportive school cultures, we have seen mentors adopt a stance of being directive and focused on remediation, falling into a patronizing or mothering role. This issue again points to the difficulty of striking a balance between maintaining a trusting relationship and supporting a new colleague to become a high-quality professional.

New mentors need support and practice to move through a mentoring conversation protocol in a natural, flowing manner; to remain sincere in helping the teacher; and to confidently rely on their own judgment and intuition. We have noted that several professional development activities support this growth, including the following:

- Observing other mentors in conversations with new teachers (in the field or on video).
- Video or audiotaping their own conversations and analyzing transcripts.
- Bringing in artifacts/data from a new teacher's practice and working with colleagues to examine and determine next steps.
- Role-playing various scenarios to practice the language.

The Mentoring Conversation Protocol is supported by the next tool that helps to promote novices' thinking about their practice and to document their professional growth.

Tool 2: Collaborative Assessment Log

The tool and its uses. The Collaborative Assessment Log is a one-page form identifying focal areas for mentoring conversations. Across the bottom of the form are teaching standards to guide goal-setting:

• Engaging and supporting all students in learning
• Creating and maintaining an effective environment
• Understanding and organizing subject matter
• Planning instruction and designing learning experiences
• Assessing student learning
• Developing as a professional educator

Each area is followed by bulleted items. The form includes four boxes for notes: What's working, Current focus-challenges-concerns; Teacher's next steps; and Mentor's next steps. Space also is provided for identifying the next meeting date and focus for that meeting.

New teachers often dwell on what is not going well and can become easily frustrated and discouraged. Their day-to-day survival mode does not allow time for reflection, nor does the culture of the profession support praising oneself for a job well done. "What's working" addresses this need. The assessment tool allows new teachers to talk through aspects of their practice with an expert other. In routine use of the log, valuable information is documented over the course of the year, and professional habits of reflection and self-assessment are established. The log is intended to be a natural part of interaction between mentor and new teacher, identifying successes and challenges and recording agreed upon ideas and next steps. These suggest a level of accountability for both parties. These sections also give the mentor opportunity to use mentoring conversation skills to help the teacher prioritize or cluster concerns, then to focus on clear and manageable changes in practice. Mentors are encouraged to take time in the last few minutes of the conversation to provide closure and build a sense of accomplishment.

Lessons learned from using the tool. Mentors with whom we work say the log is the single most valuable and versatile tool they use. Successful use of it is limited only by a mentor's ability to engage in conversation. The novice often begins in broad terms: "I'm overwhelmed." "I don't know if all my students are getting it." "I don't know what the curriculum is." The mentor guides interaction by narrowing the focus, chunking actions, and prioritizing next steps. Mentors have found the log to be a simple tool to support this work. One challenge is that the log can become mere paperwork. Mentors need to be reminded of varied methods of introducing and using the form and of using it for documentation purposes. The log itself should not drive the conversation. A paperwork focus can diminish the educative potential of mentoring.

Thoughtful examination of previous logs can inform and prepare the mentor for the next conversation, and it can provide a view of the new teacher's development over time, highlighting still challenging areas. We learned that by providing mentors with structured time to share collected logs, collaboratively analyze them, and assess their teachers' practice and the mentor's next steps, we begin to establish a habit of mind of looking at data. We find that mentors are less apt to "shoot from the hip" when problem-solving and are more apt to seriously consider evidence at hand. Also, the "Teacher's next steps" and "Mentor's next steps" build in accountability for both mentor and new teacher. Mutually, they make agreements to take actions and together they review those next steps each time they meet. One type of mentoring conversation that mentor and new teacher have involves looking at student work together. The log can be used to guide this interaction on an ongoing basis, but a more formal tool can support the novice's rigorous examination of student work and planning differentiated instructional strategies.

Tool 3: Analysis of Student Work

The tool and its uses. What can a mentor do to help focus a new teacher on student learning? Analysis of Student Work (ASW) addresses this need and helps guide instruction. ASW is both a tool and a process for mentor and new teacher to work in partnership to identify students' diverse needs related to content standards and grade-level expectations. In addition, it supports the follow-up discussion of *So what?* What do teachers do with planning and instruction once they know students' learning needs? The tool fosters conversation about differentiated instruction and provides an entry point for a mentor to share best practices from instruction. It aids in supporting novices' understanding of setting goals for students. Most important, it provides a vehicle for the novice, guided by the mentor, to channel a potentially overwhelming amount of information into patterns that become conceptual chunks of data with which to work.

Ideally, much of the time new teacher and mentor spend together involves looking at student work samples, assessing students' levels of proficiency, and planning lessons accordingly. Mentors can promote a habit of continually planning and delivering instruction based on assessed student needs—the plan, teach, reflect cycle. Overall discussions of assessment related to student learning goals and content standards include the various types of assessment tools the new teacher is using in the classroom.

For purposes of this specific, more formalized analysis, the mentor and new teacher begin by selecting a particular assessment instrument. A secondary math teacher may want to look closely at geometry placement exams, while a 1st-grade teacher may choose to analyze student writing samples as part of a districtwide assessment. Music or physical education teachers may use student performances instead of written work to analyze. Once a selection has been made, mentors ask new teachers to describe their expectations for student work. What criteria will they use to assess? Are there any established rubrics to support their assessments? Mentors might ask: What do you want your students to know? What should your students be able to do?

Once students complete the assignment, the mentor and new teacher meet to review work samples. A two-page form supports this work. The form includes identification of work selected for analysis, content standards and elements the assignment addresses, and expectations for student work/performance. Following this are four sections. The first has four columns or categories: far below standard, approaching standard, meeting standard, and exceeding standard. For each, the mentor and teacher identify "% of class." This is where they sort work into groups based on the level of meeting stated expectations or standards. Discussion during this process is important. The mentor pushes the novice to articulate reasons for a placement in terms of criteria or rubric descriptors, thus embedding the concept of using evidence to support assessment decisions. Discussion questions might include: What would you say about this student's work in relation to the criteria? What are the differences between these two students' work samples?

To scaffold the novice's learning, the next step and the second section on the form are for the teacher to identify one student from each group for in-depth analysis. The form again uses the categories related to the standard (far below, approaching, etc.). The teacher begins by describing each of four students' performances in terms of what they *can* do. Examination of student work continues to identify how students' work matches criteria, what is present and what is missing. The shift is subtle as the conversation moves toward identifying learning needs of each of the four students. The form explicitly invites this, in a section entitled "learning needs," again with columns for the four levels of performance related to the standard. Together the mentor and new teacher brainstorm specific skills, concepts, practices, or experiences each of the four students needs to progress to the next level of achievement. What have you noticed works best for this student? What crucial content gap do we need to address with this student? The natural segue is to then generate ways the new teacher can differentiate learning for these four students. The final section of the form, entitled "Differentiated Strategies," supports this. Discussion might include: various ways to group students, how learning centers could be used, what graphic organizers might be presented to support the visual learner, or how time allotments for completing specific assignments might be adjusted. To close the analysis, the mentor and new teacher identify and note on the form resources and personnel that could support either individual or groups of students.

Lessons learned from using the tool. The critical piece that emerged from our work in analyzing student work is the need to scaffold the process for new teachers. Good veteran teachers draw from years of experience, having used varied assessment instruments to determine student needs, and from accumulating their "tool kit" of instructional strategies. Novices rarely have these. They are overwhelmed by multiple needs of their students and the complexity of organizing instruction to help them. The tool and process of ASW provide a way to pull a number of pieces together by focusing in depth on four students. This, in and of itself, is valuable. However, we have found that by drawing the new teacher's attention to patterns that emerge in the study of these students in relation to the rest of the class, the mentor moves the teacher from a place of being overwhelmed to a solid understanding of the range of skills and abilities in the class. The mentor can help the novice see patterns and trends that emerge. Are there groups of students performing at a particular level, such as boys, girls, special education students, English language learners, or specific ethnic or socioeconomic groups? From here, it is much easier to organize for instruction. When we developed the ASW tool, we worked with mentors to understand its function and subtleties, and we determined when in the course of the year mentors would introduce it. Forcing its use, however, became problematic, so we began discussion of entry points, opportune moments of interaction between mentor and new teacher when it seems right to suggest ASW as a next step. We now encourage mentors to make the process organic and responsive to the teacher's interests and need to assess their students' learning.

THE MENTOR'S OPPORTUNITY TO STRENGTHEN THE PROFESSION

To develop a profession of highly qualified and caring teachers who support successful learning for all of our nation's children, mentors need tools and structures for collaborative work with novice professionals in classrooms. The best mentors know this and shoulder this responsibility with great respect. They also see this as an awesome opportunity to give something of themselves, a passing on of a legacy of good teaching. The tools are the artifacts of their craft. As Shulman (2005) noted, "Artifacts are things—objects, tools, instruments—that human beings construct because they are needed but don't exist in nature. Constructing an artifact is by definition an unnatural act. And yet . . . artifacts are the key to learning from experience" (p. 19). Through years of mentor professional development, we have found the tools described in this chapter to be among those that enable growth and learning to occur for mentors and the new teachers with whom they work.

REFERENCES

Feiman-Nemser, S. (2001). Helping novices learn to teach: Lessons from an exemplary support teacher. *Journal of Teacher Education, 52*(1), 17–30.

Glickman, C. (2002). *Leadership for learning: How to help teachers succeed.* Alexandria, VA: Association for Supervision and Curriculum Development.

Orland, L. (2001). Reading a mentoring situation: One aspect of learning to mentor. *Teaching and Teacher Education, 17*(1), 75–88.

Shulman, L. (2005). Forgive and remember: The challenges of learning from experience. In J. Gless, C. Lingman, & L. Petrock (Eds.), *Induction reader* (pp. 15–24). Santa Cruz: The New Teacher Center, University of California, Santa Cruz.

PART III

A Mentor's Knowledge of Organizational Contexts and Purposes

The organizational contexts of teachers' professional work are explored in the chapters in this part. What do mentors need to know and be able to act upon in relation to the organizational contexts and purposes of induction? A critical role of mentors is to introduce and help novices read their new school contexts, and teach them how to advocate to transform those contexts when they fail to meet the needs of students, teachers, and families. Mentors also have to navigate school and district politics and advocate on behalf of new teachers' work. Organizational and political knowledge is often new and challenging to mentors learning to see beyond the classroom walls. Further, those mentors who take on leadership roles in induction programs face additional challenges of articulating a vision of induction, building infrastructure and capacity, diagnosing challenges, and creating cultures for learning in often complicated organizational settings. Their work in this leadership domain demands new knowledge, skills, and dispositions.

The area of organizational knowledge is a particularly problematic terrain for mentors and mentor leaders who may not be familiar with issues of school reform or consider themselves powerful enough to effect change in schools and districts. The mentor's knowledge of organizational contexts and purposes demands a consciousness and disposition of advocacy that needs to be developed in mentors. The chapters in this part highlight challenges and promising practices in the area of mentors' organizational knowledge.

In Chapter 8, Wendy Baron investigates school-level contexts of novices and their implications for induction support. Drawing on survey and focus group data, Baron highlights challenging conditions of novices' work lives. The chapter describes novices' and mentors' concerns about student placement and addressing the needs of diverse learners, opportunities for collaboration with colleagues, and access to classroom and school resources. The chapter highlights actions by mentors and an induction program to address these challenging working conditions and to advocate on behalf of novices.

In Chapter 9, Betty Achinstein asks what mentors need to know and be able to do in relation to school and district contexts in order to advocate on behalf of their induction work, and what challenges mentors face in these contexts. Reporting from a study, Achinstein found that mentors need to develop "political literacy" (Kelchtermans & Ballet, 2003), an ability to "read" the organizational system. Mentors need a repertoire of strategies to navigate, respond to, advocate, and proactively influence the contexts to support their work with new teachers. Mentors also need to help new teachers learn how to read and influence their organizational contexts. The chapter highlights a case study of a mentor's political literacy in practice.

In Chapter 10, Steven Athanases and colleagues speak directly to induction program leaders as they report from two case studies of induction program development and highlight key principles and practices of leadership. One case highlights how an induction program moved from a hierarchical model to greater shared leadership, influencing the culture of the district. The other case addresses organizational challenges in a multidistrict consortium and the need for communication and coordination.

In Chapter 11, Janet Gless highlights challenges and promises when teachers become mentors of mentors. Gless draws on work with teacher induction programs in California and nationally to characterize a transformative vision of induction. The chapter offers principles that induction leaders will want to consider when defining purposes and programs: highlighting a focus on classroom practice, building collaboration and learning communities, forging new relationships with educators, and fostering educational leadership.

REFERENCE

Kelchtermans, G., & Ballet, K. (2003). Micropolitical literacy: Reconstructing a neglected dimension in teacher development. *International Journal of Educational Research, 37,* 755–767.

CHAPTER 8

Confronting the Challenging Working Conditions of New Teachers: What Mentors and Induction Programs Can Do

Wendy Baron

Novice teachers are still getting the worst assignments. They get more room changes and more special-needs students than veterans. That's the way it's always been done.

—Susan

New teachers tend to get the neediest and lowest skill-level students or low-tracked classes. They get no extra money for supplies and resources. They have little or no collegial support.

—Laura

Beginning teachers without credentials are being given the Specially Designed Academic Instruction in English classes. English language learners (ELLs) have more likelihood of having inexperienced teachers throughout the day than other "mainstreamed" students. ELLs are not getting the support in terms of language development.

—Gina

Mentors in the Making: Developing New Leaders for New Teachers, edited by Betty Achinstein and Steven Z. Athanases. Copyright © 2006 by Teachers College, Columbia University. All rights reserved. Prior to photocopying items for classroom use, please contact the Copyright Clearance Center, Customer Service, 222 Rosewood Dr., Danvers, MA 01923, USA, tel. (978) 750-8400.

As these three mentors highlight, new teachers often face the most challenging working conditions. They may rove from classroom to classroom, receive a number of different class preparations, teach a high percentage of students with special needs, and access few resources. Yet new teachers need positive working conditions in order to learn to teach and enact ambitious teaching goals. New teachers in the Santa Cruz New Teacher Project (SCNTP) identified challenging working conditions, such as not feeling prepared to teach their diverse student population, lack of collaboration with colleagues, and limited access to resources, as contributing causes to feeling ineffective (Barrett, 2002). When beginning teachers feel ineffective due to overchallenging working conditions, students may suffer. Ineffective teachers and a revolving door of new teachers cause students to lose academic ground or drop in achievement. Sanders and Rivers (1996) found that the least effective teachers produced gains of about 14 percentile points for low-achieving students during the school year, in contrast to the most effective teachers, who demonstrated gains among low–achieving students that averaged 53 percentile points.

Given the crisis in public education and our national focus on raising student achievement, we must ensure that beginning teachers are as successful as possible. Novices need assignments for which they are prepared, support from veteran colleagues and principals, and adequate resources to be effective with their students. Mentors, induction leaders, and induction programs must address the challenge of new teachers' working conditions. This chapter describes our inquiry and actions regarding this question within the SCNTP.

For 17 years, the SCNTP has advocated for working conditions that promote beginning teacher success, by working closely with district and site-level administrators and their new teachers to make them aware of inequitable practices and provide new approaches. We learned early on from new teacher surveys that combination classes (e.g., teaching 4th and 5th graders), numerous different class preparations, time-consuming duties beyond the classroom, unbalanced classes with lots of students with special needs, and lack of resources were challenging conditions that led to high stress, long hours, feelings of ineffectiveness, and eventual burnout.

Our induction program is a Beginning Teacher Support and Assessment Program with full-release mentors supporting approximately 700 new teachers each year. It is a consortium comprised of 29 districts that span 5 counties. Each district has a different policy toward supporting beginning teachers, and each school has its own unique culture, which directly influences the working conditions of new teachers. Schools in our poorest neighborhoods often have the most challenging conditions, which include lack of materials, high attrition rates among teachers, and high numbers of ELLs. Principals, superintendents, and other key educators come and go. Systems that were put in place to support novices during one administration often are lost when key people leave. Many veteran teachers are simply unwilling to reexamine or change the way "it's always been done." We find that improving the working conditions for beginning teachers is an ongoing challenge.

During the 2001–02 school year, the LNTI leadership team[1] from our program, in concert with the SCNTP Steering Committee, comprised of key people from every district, launched a yearlong inquiry into the issue of working conditions. Our goal was to identify the most challenging working conditions for novices and then target our advocacy and reform efforts. To study the question of new teacher working conditions, we conducted surveys and focus groups. Twenty-two mentors, whose mentoring represents 300 beginning teachers, responded to an open-ended questionnaire that asked them to identify the top three most challenging working conditions for their new teachers. Two hundred and thirty five beginning teachers and 78 mentors responded to open-ended questions on a midyear survey. Fifteen mentors and 10 beginning teachers also participated in two focus group discussions on working conditions.

By coding the open-ended survey responses and topics that surfaced in focus groups, we categorized the dominant challenging working conditions. We devised a thematic code so we could cluster related conditions. We did a cross-data comparison of the two data sets, looking for patterns, similarities, and differences. To support our analysis, we created a matrix comparing responses from mentors and beginning teachers.

CHALLENGING WORKING CONDITIONS

Three central themes emerged from data analysis:

1. Challenges in meeting the needs of diverse learners.
2. Lack of collaboration with colleagues.
3. Poor resources, materials, and classroom and school conditions.[2]

First, both novices and mentors identified how new teachers feel unprepared to work with students at different levels, especially those below grade level, with ELLs, and with special population students. They often lack the classroom management skills, resources, materials, and professional development to differentiate instruction. Particularly, novices reported struggling with differentiating instruction and understanding ways to tailor curriculum to the wide range of learning needs in their classrooms. They cited a lack of support in assessing students' language and reading levels as well as a need for more support in communicating with non-English-proficient students. Moreover, many new teachers reported having more ELLs and special education students than they felt prepared to teach. Mentors overwhelmingly reported that their new teachers were placed with challenging English learners and special-needs students without appropriate preparation or resources. This finding raises important concerns. New teachers who feel unprepared to work with English learners and special needs students are less likely to be effective with those students than teachers who are prepared. To meet our national achievement goals, students must be assigned to teachers most qualified to meet their language and special needs. Novices need to be placed in appropriate assignments and provided with sufficient professional development and resources to teach their students. Working with English learners and special needs students is challenging for the most seasoned veteran teachers, and even more so for novices.

Second, new teachers reported a sense of isolation and a longing for collaboration with colleagues. They reported that their schools did not provide enough structures or time for such a collaborative culture to emerge. They reported a lack of structures to support collaborative planning, teaching, and discussion of student work. New teachers identified that they wanted these opportunities and were looking for a learning community. Others reported unsupportive colleagues involved in their own work with little time to reach out to newcomers. This finding also raises concerns for novices. Teachers are traditionally isolated from one another. Staff, department, and grade-level meetings are often business-oriented, not a time for teachers to collaborate, share, and learn together. Management-oriented principals tend to foster a top-down, rather than collaborative, school culture. Yet beginning teachers want and need collegial support and a school culture that fosters collaboration. The fact that new teachers cite the need to collaborate tells us that they want and need support in order to be successful in this complex and demanding role. As schools become learning communities where teachers analyze student work, talk about instructional practices, and think together about how to meet the learning needs of all students, beginning teachers will have a greater chance of being effective during their first few years.

Third, novices and mentors reported a lack of resources and materials and poor classroom and school conditions as challenges. The beginning teachers identified not having appropriate amounts and quality of materials and supplies to meet the needs of their students. Furthermore, the physical condition of their classrooms and schools was problematic. While some reported not having their own classroom and roving to multiple settings, others were located in portables far away from the campus center or grade-level colleagues. Mentors and novices remarked on the substandard classrooms filled with junk, missing supplies, or furniture. Building sites were decrepit or did not provide enough space for expanding populations. Moreover, mentors and new teachers identified a lack of money for supplies and books.

This inequitable distribution of resources, with new teachers at the short end, raises major concerns. Often the reason for such practices is tradition. In the mentor focus group, we learned that veteran teachers often feel entitled to certain privileges. Veterans get very few acknowledgments or privileges for their years of service. Having a good classroom and adequate resources and teaching the advanced classes sometimes becomes that acknowledgment. Most veteran teachers had to sink or swim when they entered the profession and have "paid their dues" over the years. New teachers need such vital resources, materials, and classroom conditions to provide a quality education to their students. They, even more so than their veteran colleagues, need as many resources at their disposal as they can get. Many times, new teachers either do not know to question the kinds of conditions in which they enter teaching or are not comfortable speaking out for more equitable conditions.

WHAT MENTORS AND INDUCTION PROGRAMS CAN DO

The SCNTP's Leadership Team and Steering Committee used data from this study to determine three working conditions to target for improvement: being prepared to work with ELLs and special population students, collaborating at the school site with veteran colleagues, and ensuring that teachers have the supplies and materials they need. We acknowledged that schools need policies to ensure that new teachers are assigned appropriately and have balanced classes, limited numbers of preps, and the resources they need to be effective with a wide range of student learning needs. We believe that when schools are organized into learning communities, instructional capacity is better distributed among members.

Being Prepared to Work with English Learners and Special Population Students

Providing ongoing professional development to beginning teachers and mentors to improve their effectiveness in working with ELLs and special population students was our first task. The SCNTP established an ELL Institute in collaboration with the Pajaro Unified School District and the University of California, Santa Cruz Teacher Education Program for new teachers and their mentors. The professional development series was facilitated by mentor leaders in the induction program, and external experts joined some of the workshops. Ninety people participated, including beginning teachers and their mentors, who were required to come as part of mentor professional development. It was recommended for all 2nd-year new teachers, and 1st-year teachers were invited. Twenty other veteran teachers from the district participated. Since the piloting of the institute, we now have integrated this work projectwide. Currently, all new teachers in our project participate in a series of professional development workshops on working with ELLs.

In the ELL Institute, we focused our learning on language acquisition, English Language Development (ELD) strategies, differentiating instruction, and ensuring access to content. Novices and their mentors were expected to analyze student work on a regular basis and plan lessons using differentiation strategies to meet the learning needs of the students. The facilitators of the ELL Institute also provided a historical context for the participating teachers. The first two workshops focused on the state of ELLs, including statistics about the rise in numbers of ELLs in California and their achievement levels and dropout rates compared to other cultural groups. Also included in the first workshop were information on language learning and the stages of language acquisition. The third and fourth workshops focused on the differences between primary and secondary language development. Participants were introduced to ELD strategies and models. The notion of action research was introduced, and beginning, veteran, and mentor teachers were asked to think about questions they had about their teaching and student learning as related to language development. Later in the Institute, teachers and mentors learned about developing academic language and began planning their action research. Participants engaged in action research, applying strategies learned in the ELL Institute, analyzing student work, and reflecting on practice. Mentors followed up on learning from the ELL Institute during on-site meetings with beginning teachers, and problem-solved dilemmas and challenges related to ELLs. Other topics, such as "What Makes Reading Text Difficult?" and research-based instructional strategies, supported continued growth of participants. Later on, mentors and beginning and veteran teachers again analyzed student work to measure action research progress. The closing colloquium focused on action research presentations, during which time teachers shared promising practices and dilemmas.

Our special education mentors created and implemented *a Teaching Special Population Students* seminar series in which all beginning teachers and mentors participate. The purpose of this series is to understand laws and requirements of special education students so that new teachers can see that it is within their realm of responsibility to support special needs students and provide them with a means of support. Observations of special population students, analyzing student work, and planning differentiated lessons are helping prepare beginning teachers to work with diverse learners and build professional habits of planning based on assessment of student learning needs.

Mentors are facilitating collaboration with special educators and other resource personnel so that it is becoming a norm rather than an exception. The series addresses a number of key questions in the field:

- What is the special education system?
- What is a student's Individual Education Plan?
- How do we refer students to the student study team process?
- How do we access needed resources?
- What are the students' legal rights?
- What are my responsibilities?
- How can we collaborate with special educators?
- How will we differentiate for special education?
- What kinds of accommodations or modifications for students are appropriate?

In addition, the series highlights a teacher-development-continuum rubric for teachers to assess themselves in meeting needs of special populations.

In the past 2 years several districts in the SCNTP consortium have begun providing integrated professional development and coaching support to all teachers in literacy and ELD. Some of the districts are providing on-site ELD coaching to new and veteran teachers, as well as to bilingual resource teachers, to ensure meeting the needs of ELLs. One district, our largest and most rural, has marshaled the efforts of every administrator and teacher leader to development on-site ELD networks and coaching support for all teachers on English language development. These change efforts have been led by several of the district's administrative representatives on the SCNTP Steering Committee.

Collaborating at the School Site with Veteran Colleagues

Creating cultures of collaboration among teachers is even more removed from our induction program's area of immediate influence. We are an outside organization, and yet we employ our participating districts' teachers to mentor their novices. Thus, our mentors are important agents in influencing changes in school culture. It takes district, principal, and teacher leaders to have vision and do the work involved in creating schools as learning communities for adults. Thus, we take a long-range, multipronged approach to improving this working condition.

We have offered our mentors as facilitators of on-site professional development, so many mentors in the SCNTP are now facilitating grade-level, department, and staff meetings on analyzing student work and differentiating instruction for various student learning needs. During their meetings with principals, mentors talk about their work with beginning teachers and share our formative assessment tools. Principals are seeing the value of our ambitious mentoring model. In some districts, mentors have worked with principals to offer professional development opportunities for the whole staff (e.g., assessment strategies).

We also support mentors to co-lead professional development with veterans in the schools and districts with whom we have worked. For example, in two of our districts, a mentor has integrated the veteran and new teacher professional development. New teachers attend all professional development series with veterans. Mentors continue to support new teachers in other areas. In another district, mentors are part of larger professional development efforts, providing learning opportunities for veterans and novices alike (e.g., in lesson study). In this district, the new teachers will combine their induction work of analyzing student work during their district lesson study project with veterans. Other districts are not yet focused on collaboration and developing learning communities. In some sites, there are challenges that make building a collaborative culture difficult.

In 2002–03, SCNTP mentors at a rural middle school with a large ELL population were asked to work with the entire language arts team. At first, their role was undefined. However, with input from staff, they began establishing professional habits that include analyzing student work, planning differentiated lessons, and observing one another. The mentors offer workshops on ELD strategies, vocabulary development, comprehension, fluency, writing, and so forth when requested by the language arts teachers. These professional development needs often arise as a result of analyzing student work and planning lessons. Mentors continue work with new teachers at the site, 1½ hours a week, as is the custom of our program. These two mentors have been influential in building a collaborative culture at the site, as well as in preparing all teachers to work with diverse learners.

As a result of our offer to principals, some mentors are facilitating staff meetings focused on analyzing a specific assessment. In this case the mentor brings together grade-level or department teams to analyze students' work, discuss their learning needs, and share differentiation strategies. When the special education and bilingual resource teachers are part of this conversation, collaboration among general, special, and bilingual educators is a natural outcome. We are finding this strategy is effective in promoting dialogue and collaboration among teachers and leads to a more focused improvement plan schoolwide.

Sometimes we influence culture through an intervention. At one rural high school of 2,000 students, a new teacher had five different class preparations and moved to three different classrooms over the course of a day. Her department rarely met to plan together or discuss students. The beginning teacher felt isolated and was uncomfortable asking her colleagues for help. The mentor talked at length with the principal and assistant principals about the working conditions of this and other beginning teachers on campus. The mentor cited the attrition rate of teachers at that site, and spoke about the importance of setting up the environment so novices are close to their veteran colleagues and have limited numbers of preps and roving. She also advocated for department collaboration as a way to support beginning teachers. By the 2nd year of advocating for a change in conditions, a shift happened. First, the administrators got agreement from the staff to reconfigure the classrooms so departments would be located together. Next, all beginning teachers saw a decline in numbers of preps and classrooms. Additionally, department chairs facilitate a weekly collaboration time among teachers in that department.

As funds for induction shrink, we think that our new strategy has many systemwide as well as cost benefits. When the whole staff participates in learning and assessing together, the beginning teacher becomes part of a larger learning community and is better prepared to work with diverse learners in their context. This might even mean less one-to-one time with the mentor is needed, as the beginning teacher fulfills some program requirements during the on-site collaboration time. A bonus is that the principals are supported in their instructional leadership as well.

Ensuring That Teachers Have the Resources They Need

Since the No Child Left Behind (NCLB) legislation was enacted, we have noticed a concerted effort among participating districts to provide materials, texts, teacher manuals, and other resources, such as ELD supplemental materials, to all teachers. Most districts have adopted a particular language arts text, and a variety of materials are provided to each teacher, including resources to challenge students and meet the needs of ELLs.

Although NCLB has had an effect on one target working condition, the SCNTP's Leadership Team is continuing to develop a more systematic approach to improving access to resources and materials for novices. SCNTP mentors discussed and learned how to advocate for improvements in beginning teacher working conditions and to support new teachers in asserting themselves to advocate for their own needs. We developed a protocol and tool that mentors now use to plan and conduct conversations with principals about their work with new teachers. Prior to their monthly meeting with the principal, the new teacher and his or her mentor discuss the new teacher's needs. They frame the conversation in terms of creating the most supportive environment for quality teaching. Then they turn to expectations of working conditions, often identifying specific resources needed. For example, if a beginning teacher needs a file cabinet, lab equipment, or other support with a class, it is documented on the Administrator–Mentor Conversation Log. Either the mentor then raises the issues during the monthly check-in with the principal, or the beginning teacher asks the principal directly for the particular materials or resources needed.

Mentors receive professional development in communicating with principals. They role-play conversations involving advocating for improved working conditions for new teachers. This monthly check-in with the principal has had a dramatic effect on ensuring that new teachers have resources and materials they need. Moreover, the mentor acts as advocate and ongoing reminder to the principal to ensure quality working conditions. Most principals are very receptive to material/resource needs and somehow find the necessary money for purchases of supplemental materials, texts, supplies, and so on. However, systems to ensure that beginning teachers have the resources and materials they need at the start of the school year are in place at only a few schools.

Beyond directly advocating with principals, the Project has focused on empowering new teachers to talk to administrators and to seek out school and community resources they need. As part of their mentoring exchanges, novices utilize a tool that helps them identify personnel, programs, facilities, and resources within their school and larger community that support their students' needs. In this way, the mentoring program enables the novice to develop an inventory of resources in terms of supplies, resource teachers, grants, community-based programs, support providers, and parent liaisons to support their teaching. Furthermore, mentors role-play with new teachers the kinds of interactions they may encounter with site administrators in asserting their access to appropriate resources. New teachers thus learn skills and language of empowerment.

FUTURE DIRECTIONS FOR FOSTERING POSITIVE NEW TEACHER WORKING CONDITIONS

We have targeted the mentor as an agent of change and induction as the lever. The SCNTP is investing in professional development for mentors, building their skills as facilitators, coaches, and leaders. As teacher leaders, mentors have a huge influence on the systems of school. All mentors in our project are asked to share data about working conditions with district administrators, board members, and teacher union groups. Mentors give new teachers a powerful voice by promoting equitable practices.

Our organization can influence change in working conditions for novices most effectively if we support development of sustainable learning communities focused on analyzing student work and instruction. Collaboration will lead to discussions about resources and supplies. Veterans will hear about the needs of the beginning teachers and advocate for their support. As working conditions improve, beginning teachers will feel more effective with their students. Effective teachers impact student achievement. I am hopeful. Over the past 16 years, our project has supported over 3,500 new teachers and 200 mentor teachers. Many former beginning teachers and mentors are now content coaches, union leaders, assistant principals, and principals. The experience they have had with our professional development practices carries into the field. New norms of collaboration, inquiry, research, and professionalism take shape in various contexts. Building capacity has become the goal. We are moving an area of concern into an area of influence. Induction is not enough if we are only doing good work one-on-one with beginning teachers. The big work is to create systems that support teacher learning and development on site, as a matter of everyday life.

NOTES

1. Wendy Baron, Trinidad Castro, Leslie Smith, Colleen Stobbe, Linda St. John, and Betsy Warren made up the LNTI leadership team. We also acknowledge the support of Adele Barrett in survey analysis.
2. Other issues included: challenges with administrators, lack of support in instruction, combination classrooms, roving between classrooms, students not at grade level, behavior problem students, and overcrowded classrooms and schools.

REFERENCES

Barrett, A. (2002). *New Teacher Induction Survey*. Santa Cruz, CA: The New Teacher Center at the University of California, Santa Cruz.
Sanders, W., & Rivers, J. (1996). *Cumulative and residual effects of teachers on future academic achievement*. Knoxville: University of Tennessee Value-Added Research and Assessment Center.

CHAPTER 9

Mentors' Organizational and Political Literacy in Negotiating Induction Contexts

Betty Achinstein

> My mentor has really helped me out when it comes to the politics in this school.
>
> —Rob, a new teacher

> I've realized I first need to figure out how the system operates and then teach the beginning teachers how it operates. I'm having to learn the system to teach them the system. I've also had to be an advocate for Rob. That's been my role, which is different than what I thought coaching would be.
>
> —Maya, Rob's mentor

New teachers, like Rob, often enter schools with little knowledge of organizations and the politics of school life.[1] The "practice shock" (Veenman, 1984) they experience has to do with their transition to teaching students, but also with their socialization into schools as they face conflicts with colleagues, administrators, and policies. New teachers' beliefs and actions may conflict with existing organizational norms, and they face issues of power, interest, and negotiation. One job of mentors such as Maya is to learn how to help new teachers read their school contexts. Mentors also need to know how to navigate school and district cultures to advocate on behalf of their new teachers' work lives. Finally, they need to support the development of new teachers' own political knowledge and ability to advocate for themselves.

Yet oftentimes mentors come to their positions with little knowledge of complex contexts beyond classrooms, or an assumption that navigating such political terrains and advocating for change within a system are not part of their role. Districts rarely provide the support induction leaders need to negotiate organizational contexts beyond the classroom. Participants in The Leadership Network for Teacher Induction (LNTI, see the Introduction) identified this struggle as taking on a leadership role in an unfamiliar political environment. The mentors and induction leaders began identifying their lack of "political awareness," their challenge not only to "read" the system within which they worked, but then to navigate it, and ultimately to transform it. This chapter explores the political and organizational contexts of mentoring and induction, asking: (1) What do mentors need to know and be able to do in relation to school and district contexts in order to advocate on behalf of their induction work? (2) What are the challenges mentors face in their school and district contexts? I use the expertise of 31 induction leaders (veteran mentors and induction directors in LNTI) documented in open-ended questionnaire responses. I also include an intensive case study of mentoring practice selected from a larger sample of mentor–novice case studies of an induction network program. The case was selected because it most directly addressed the dimensions of political literacy identified in the questionnaire analysis, and it raised challenges to enacting such a knowledge base worthy of investigation. The mentor in the case also was explicitly involved in induction work addressing a whole-school reform initiative.[2]

POLITICAL LITERACY

Recent research on novices identifies a need to analyze power, influence, conflict, and control inside new teachers' organizational contexts, offering a micropolitical perspective. Kelchtermans & Ballet (2002, 2003) define how teachers learn to "read" micropolitical reality and "write" themselves into it as micropolitical literacy.[3] This literacy has three aspects: (1) an ability to acknowledge, interpret, and understand ("see" and "read") the micropolitics of a situation; (2) an instrumental or operational dimension involving strategies teachers apply to address issues; and (3) an awareness of satisfaction or dissatisfaction the teacher experiences as a result of his/her political literacy. The political reality of schools promotes vulnerability, anger, guilt, or satisfaction (Kelchtermans & Ballet, 2002).

While some research has examined political knowledge and strategies new teachers need to develop, little has examined mentors' political literacy. Teachers' political strategies may fall along a spectrum from reactive to proactive (Blase, 1988; Goodman, 1988). Teachers' micropolitical actions may be more cyclical in nature, beginning as action to restore lost conditions but becoming proactive in strategies to change the situation (Kelchtermans & Ballet, 2002). But what supports novices to learn such a repertoire, to adopt political lenses? What knowledge, skills, and dispositions do *mentors* need for political literacy?

IDENTIFYING A MENTOR'S ORGANIZATIONAL AND POLITICAL KNOWLEDGE

Participants identified three critical domains of mentors' knowledge of political and organizational contexts: reading, navigating, and advocating. In each domain, respondents reported that mentors need knowledge, skills, and commitments themselves and the ability to foster these in new teachers.

As Figure 9.1 shows, 90% of respondents reported that such a knowledge base of contexts requires that mentors *read the organizational and political system*, which includes knowledge and understanding of cultures and systems, key participants, and political processes in schools and districts. This domain also involves developing such political lenses in novices as well. Enabling novices to "see the bigger picture" and "know the unspoken rules" are the mentors' responsibility. One LNTI respondent explained: "It is very difficult for someone immersed in a culture to analyze the aspects of it. It often takes a fresh set of eyes to see what goes on at a school that is taken for granted by the people who 'live' there." Another reported the need to show novices others' perspectives: "My new teachers have been in tears over adult-to-adult relationships and teaming conflicts. Getting these new teachers to 'see' department issues, school change outside their classroom, and a principal's point of view and needs, has been a significant part of our talk." Another aspect of "reading" involves the mentor and novice examining their own beliefs, as one respondent explained: "A leader cannot lead without knowing deeply about herself. Knowing one's political beliefs and values will help illuminate the similarities (or differences) that exist in a given context. Being politically savvy means being able to understand the core values of all involved in a situation (the mentor, the novice, the school, and the district values)."

Figure 9.1 shows that 71% of respondents reported a second domain as the mentors' need for a repertoire of strategies to *navigate challenges of or-*

Figure 9.1. Mentors' Organizational and Political Knowledge

	Number (and percentage) of respondents reporting (n = 31)
Read organizational and political contexts	28 (90%)
Read systems: Build knowledge and understanding of organizational structures, processes, systems, and problems	25 (81%)
Read others: Develop ability to read key players, needs and interests, and power	12 (39%)
Help novices read: Guide new teachers to read contexts	5 (16%)
Read self: Demonstrate disposition to examine one's own beliefs, values, and role in relation to the organization	2 (7%)
Navigate challenges within organizations	22 (71%)
Develop repertoire of strategies and skills to manage immediate problems (e.g., foster communication, build relationships, become respected)	20 (65%)
Marshal resources	5 (16%)
Guide new teachers to navigate challenging contexts	4 (13%)
Advocate for change	16 (52%)
Advocate for/Influence change	11 (36%)
Understand the change process	5 (16%)
Guide new teachers to advocate for themselves	3 (10%)

ganizational contexts "diplomatically" and to develop such skills in new teachers. Respondents identified the capacity to negotiate problematic situations, primarily through communication, developing strong relationships with key participants, becoming respected at the site, and marshaling resources. One participant explained how she needed to: "find resources from other districts, assemble meetings of key players including a Special Education mentor from another district, get our Induction Director involved . . . in order to help support the needs of special education new teachers and their mentors." Another described how a new teacher fell out of favor with the site administrator and how the mentor had to support the new teacher to "concentrate on his lesson planning and student achievement, so [the principal] couldn't give him negative evaluations."

The third major domain, identified by 52% of respondents, is that mentors need knowledge of how to *advocate for change* and an ability to foster self-advocacy in new teachers. One member described a novice 2nd-grade teacher as having:

> eight resource students, one fully included physically disabled student, two GATE [gifted] students, and nine "middle-level" students. Her grade-level team was friendly but uninterested in working with her. The parent community was hypervigilant; one parent became verbally abusive. It was necessary to involve a rather uninterested administrator in her support. The new teacher and I planned out our "connection" with the principal *together* ahead of time. When *we* approached the principal, it was a partner approach to obtain better working conditions for her.

The following case study examines the complexity of using these domains of political literacy to support new teachers' worklives.

MAYA AND ROB: A CASE STUDY OF POLITICAL LITERACY

Rob was a white new teacher in his early 20s teaching 5th grade in a low-income, low-performing, and high-minority elementary school. The district and school were under great scrutiny for their low-performing status. Rob was assigned a mentor, Maya, who met with him as part of a whole-school reform initiative that targeted supporting new teachers schoolwide. Maya, a veteran elementary school teacher, literacy resource specialist, and mentor, worked in a different district from Rob. Along with Rob, Maya was coming to learn how to navigate the culture of Rob's district and school.

Two major conflicts arose for Rob in his 1st year of teaching. In both cases, Maya actively read, navigated, and advocated on behalf of Rob, supporting him in learning to become more politically literate. Both conflicts raised serious challenges for Maya in her role as mentor, in relation to Rob and the school.

Conflict About the Literacy Curriculum

To address their "low-performing" status and district/state scrutiny, Rob's district and school developed an improvement plan that adopted the state-sanctioned literacy program, Open Court (2005). The program was identified by all participants as "highly prescriptive," including 10 teacher guides per set, pacing guidelines, and an emphasis on "teacher-directed instruction," and phonics-based learning using an anthology. Rob's school purchased too few text sets, leaving many teachers without texts, others with outdated ones. The district later also adopted the state-approved High Point (for students 2 or more years below grade level) (2005). Rob remarked:

> You could teach Open Court your whole life and I guess get paid to be a teacher. You can walk in, do almost no prep and teach it. . . . But [my kids] were not learning from it and they were not finding any fun in it . . . I thought the stories were poor . . . [and the] activities had low expectations.

To make it meaningful, Rob felt, "you should design the program around your students, not the students around a program." He said, "I don't know if this is just a power issue, but I don't enjoy being told what to do every day, and that is how I felt when I was teaching Open Court." A month into the school year, Rob said, "If I do it all year, and next year, and the year after . . . I'll tell you right now, I'm going to drop out of teaching. . . . I want to throw out Open Court."

His convictions about how to teach literacy included a "balanced approach," developing a community of learners where students engaged in dialogue, and focusing on novels (rather than anthologies) and literature study. Rob wanted to approach his principal, Brenda, about his concerns and propose an alternative literature-based approach, which would still teach to state standards. He wanted to collaborate closely with his mentor and Lisa, a new grade-level colleague. He wanted to hand over his set of Open Court texts to a teacher who wanted them, and he would agree to accept the High Point texts when they came in and would use them one day a week for grammar work. Although the principal had observed Rob's literature-based class and liked what she had seen, she was under district and state scrutiny to follow the improvement plan and adopted curriculum. As an untenured teacher without a clear credential, Rob took a risk in challenging the status quo. Maya worked closely with him, other new teachers, the principal, and the district to negotiate this challenge.

Read organizational and political contexts. Maya and Rob *read the system,* realizing they needed to learn about the district organizational context promoting the literacy curriculum. Maya went to Open Court trainings and examined the district's position in adopting a state-sponsored, funded, and heavily prescriptive program. She understood it as part of the culture of a district under state scrutiny and clearly read the pressures the school faced moving out of its "underperforming status." Similarly, Rob expressed, "I was skeptical that I was going to be able to get away with not teaching this program because it's in our improvement plan. The school was on the brink of being taken over by the state because our scores were so low."

Maya worked with Rob to *read others*, understanding the principal's political position. In one mentoring conference, Maya explained, "The principal is very proud of what you and Lisa are doing. So hold onto that. Also, know that she's playing the political game, too. She's got her [district-level] administration . . . she has to play all the angles, too." In an interview, the principal, Brenda, explained, "We're going to have a state compliance review. We use these funds for textbooks and Rob's not using the state adopted texts. . . . So I'm pressuring him that yes, we have to be compliant." Still, Brenda sympathized with Rob's teaching approaches, knowing his students were engaged. This was an awkward position: "The conflict now is within me." While Rob came to feel supported by his principal, he realized her political constraints: "She has her hands tied. . . . I know she doesn't bug me about it but that she just wants to make it apparent that if someone asks, that I have all the materials in my room. I think she's just covering her bases."

Maya helped Rob to *read (him)self* in challenging the literacy program. Rob explained that Maya "taught me to be passionate; when you are asking for something, to show how much you want it." Maya explained that she told new teachers to "trust what is right in your heart. . . . If you're doing it because someone is telling you you have to, then you're not going to stay in this profession long. You have to hold to your true values. If you don't then the profession dies." She explained that it was important not to offend anybody, but to hold onto "what you know is good pedagogy." She urged Rob to "read himself" as "a teacher with conviction."

Negotiate the challenges. Maya explained how it was vital to *find political allies and build relationships.* She was educating teachers about:

> What the politics are and how to play the politics, what people's roles are, who holds the power, and who we want to make happy. If you make your principal happy, she'll advocate for you. I told Rob, "Brenda will advocate for you if you keep her on your side. Then you don't have to worry as much about up there [the district level]."

Rob began to work closely with Lisa, who shared commitments to balanced literacy approaches. They began to co-construct curriculum, planning daily and sharing resources. They bolstered each other in grade-level meetings and became strong advocates for one another.

Rob realized he could *marshal resources* as a political leverage. When he approached the principal, he explained that since there were not enough Open Court textbook sets, he would be willing to hand over his to another grade-level teacher who wanted it. The literature-based approach Rob wanted to utilize required purchasing novels the school did not have. Because there were no school resources, he sought an external grant of $1,000 to purchase novels for himself and Lisa. Maya and her induction organization also worked with a foundation to secure funds and purchase materials for a book room to promote literature study.

Maya supported Rob to *become respected* by teaching him strategies about "balanced literacy" approaches, including shared and guided reading and interactive writing. She sought resources so Rob could attend a literacy professional development conference. She took him to observe three expert teachers in other districts so he would have the vision of what was possible. She taught him that he would need to "teach to the standards" and document his successes, that this would earn him respect, avoiding negative attention. Maya explained, "I tell the new teachers, 'It's very political . . . So if you can show results, that you're teaching those standards, that's what matters." Ultimately, Rob's and Lisa's classes scored the highest grades at their grade level on a district reading assessment. This was announced at a district-level meeting.

Advocate for change. Rob knew Maya went to speak to district administrators on his behalf, seeking allies and promoting new thinking about literacy. "She was checking out for me, would it be okay if a teacher comes up with his own lessons. The administrator said, as long as it is linked to the standards." Maya, along with her induction leader colleagues, presented literacy ideas to district administrators and school board members that inspired discussions of alternative approaches. Maya recognized that one administrator was deeply invested in the district's program, but that another administrator and a school board member were on her side. Maya assured Rob that "We were talking at the higher levels, where we kind of infiltrated, talked about the coaching process and literacy . . . we're working on it from different angles."

Challenges. Maya had to proceed with care, needing to sustain relationships with the principal, school, and district. She recognized that she would "try to keep it very safe and play the politics because we don't want to come in as outsiders and tell them what to do." She identified that "Rob is doing exactly what I wish all new teachers would do—going out and speaking his mind . . . not just becoming complacent and thinking that all these mandates have to happen to us." She also expressed concern: "But I feel that I'm in an odd situation because I want to empower him and I am empowering him. But I know I have to play the politics."

While Rob continued to implement his approach to literacy, he and Maya faced new challenges in Rob's second year of teaching. A new superintendent emphasized greater fidelity to the Open Court program and thus put tighter constraints on Rob and Maya. Maya sought to continue to support Rob's alternative literacy approaches, strengthen his practices, and let him know there were other "pockets of resistance" in the school and district. She also tried to help Rob accommodate some of the school's literacy program practices while still sustaining his own approaches in order to keep him from getting into administrative trouble. The conflicts about literacy practices continued as shifts in district policies occurred over time.

Maya also admitted that the focus on this conflict may have taken away from a focus on teaching. "Because we spent so much time navigating the district issues it pulled away from Rob having to look deeply at himself as a reflective teacher." All the focus on the politics of change created a high level of stress for the novices and Maya: "Always navigating through [this school] is really difficult because their stress levels are so high and I never fathomed all of this incredible stress for me."

Conflict About Student Tracking

Rob's grade-level team consisted of three 1st-year teachers, a 2nd-year temporary and uncredentialed teacher, and one 12-year veteran, Sue, who wielded great power. A conflict arose when Sue decided the 5th-grade team should be "leveled" based on "ability" and test scores. She found some students "too low" for the Open Court materials. Sue wanted to remove her 11 lowest students from her class and spread them between the two new teachers' classrooms, wanting to keep the "higher students" for herself and using the Open Court materials. Rob believed the 11 she selected were also "problem students behaviorally." Rob disagreed with this approach, explaining:

> That's ability grouping and that goes against everything that I've ever learned in education, especially when it's the entire class. . . . This can't be right. . . . I just thought this would be so detrimental to the 5th grade if we ability grouped the entire grade. I thought it was illegal to track.

Rob wanted to confront Sue and his principal on this issue. He told Sue, "It's not that I don't want to follow your directions, it's just I think that by moving all the students out of your class and putting them into our classes, is not the right way to go about it." Rob explained that Sue replied that she was not going to change her ways; Rob then met with the principal.

The principal, in trying to understand Sue's position, said in an interview, "The kids should be leveled because it makes it easier for the teacher not to have this range of levels when the class is very difficult." After Rob's initial encounter with the principal, he walked out so upset that he called Maya to say, "We have to have a sit-down [meeting]. I want to know if I'm just out of my mind or do you think this is wrong?" Maya said, "Rob, I'm totally with you on this. I am going to fight this." Maya then worked at two levels of political literacy. She *guided Rob in how to be a self-advocate*, supporting his political literacy and capacity not only to navigate, but to challenge the system. Maya also sought to navigate and *advocate on behalf of Rob* about the tracking conflict.

Mentor guiding new teacher to self-advocate. Rob explained how his mentor coached him through "heated grade-level meetings" on the tracking debate: "Sometimes you need extra support when you are disagreeing with somebody, and she was present at many grade-level meetings. During the heat of it, when it was really ugly, she didn't miss a single one . . . and she was coaching me through it."

Maya and Rob debriefed one grade-level meeting where the principal, Brenda, and Maya were also in attendance. The mentoring excerpt captures Maya's role in teaching Rob to be a self-advocate. In the opening excerpt we see how Maya supported Rob to know his philosophical beliefs and to stand by his moral commitments. This supported Rob to articulate his professional beliefs to guide future actions in advocating against tracking practices he deemed unethical [M = Mentor; T = Teacher].

> T: I'm glad you came [to the meeting]. . . . It was the most heated debate that I've ever been in in my life . . . when Sue was saying that we weren't thinking of our students. I don't know how anyone in their right mind can say that. . . . I'm trying to find the right way that I think students should be educated. . . .
>
> M: I was trying to think of ways to help you, too. I was proud of you that you held your ground, what you know is best for students. You're holding onto your philosophy.

The conversation continued with Maya identifying her own precarious role as an outsider to the school, and challenging Rob to be a change agent who could work within the system: "You know I have to be very careful politically; a little more careful than you because I'm coming in as kind of an outsider. . . . You're the ones that are going to be here and changing things if they can be possibly changed."

Maya then used strategies to bolster Rob's powers to advocate for himself. First, she provided Rob with relevant literature on differentiating instruction for heterogeneous classrooms to "empower his voice": "I told you about this book by Carol Tomlinson [1998]. I will bring you a little chapter or two at a time. This will be good for you as you're speaking to be more empowered; you can speak to specifics and speak to the theory."

Second, she identified for Rob negative consequences in low-tracked classrooms: "The teacher that has the 'bottom of the barrel,' they're not just dealing with struggling readers, but with the struggling behaviors, emotional issues, these kids see themselves as maybe failures. It's much more complex than just putting them at these various levels."

Third, she encouraged Rob to document successes with his untracked class. This scripted evidence could empower Rob when "talking to a strong personality" and could serve Maya in negotiating with "upper administration."

Mentor's advocacy. Maya tried to "read" the principal's position, realizing Brenda needed information because she came from an upper-elementary-grade background, lacked literacy expertise, and was unclear about differences between flexible grouping for reading and rigid homogeneous tracking.

Maya took an advocacy stance with the principal, educating and influencing. Yet she acknowledged the complexity of challenging the principal and a veteran teacher so early in her relationship with the school: "We didn't want to turn Brenda off by pushing too much. So we had to play that politically really carefully. . . . I'm trying to maintain that relationship because I know that if I don't, there's no hope for subversive sabotage or infiltrating." Maya's approach with both Brenda and Sue involved "a careful walking the edges, feeling them out, and understanding where they are coming from." Maya explained how she approached the principal with a nonadversarial stance:

> I asked her an open-ended question. I said, "Can you tell me about Rob?" I approached it from a mentor's point of view. "My job is to support. I really want to be an advocate for Rob and he's really concerned about these kids being moved into classes based on their reading level and you know that's tracking. You know the research shows that once a child's in a classroom with all the same level of kids, that the high ones are going to fly, regardless, but the struggling ones, they stay low."

Maya explained the difference between a whole class being grouped according to their level and a class having heterogeneous groupings where you can pull in flexible homogeneous groups. She offered to work with all the teachers on strategies for differentiating instruction within heterogeneous untracked classrooms. In her work with Sue, Maya tried to raise questions about the efficacy of the approach. "Our very subtle pressure, in an informational and questioning style, made [Sue] think twice and wonder."

The tracking issue resolved over time. The veteran did not end up moving 11 students. Rob did take two of Sue's students. She also sent a few to the other new teachers' classrooms. Rob and his mentor felt the situation was resolved without tracking the whole grade.

THE ORGANIZATIONAL KNOWLEDGE BASE OF MENTORING

This chapter highlights mentors' knowledge of organizational contexts in three domains of political literacy: reading, navigating, and advocating. In each, respondents identified how mentors need to proceed on two levels: developing their own knowledge and fostering it in new teachers. The case of Maya and Rob highlights the complexity of the political terrain for both novices and mentors. The case also demonstrates how mentors must be "political animals," working up, down, and across systems on behalf of new teachers, as well as supporting novices to self-advocate.

A Challenging Role for Mentors

A mentor in Maya's induction program expressed a mentoring challenge: "We're all clear that our role is to support our new teachers to navigate the system they are in, but it's not clear whether our role is to support our teachers *to change* the system." The mentor's role is often seen as easing the transition of novices into the current system (status quo), rather than criticizing schooling practices, challenging tracking, critiquing district curricular choices, and confronting colleagues. This raises questions about the appropriate role of mentors as local guides or critical change agents. Wang and Odell (2002) reviewed various assumptions of mentoring programs, including a humanistic perspective (help novices deal with reality shock); a situated apprentice perspective (technical support); and critical constructivist perspective (learn to teach for social justice). Feiman-Nemser (2001) similarly contrasts mentoring stances, including: "local guide," "educational companion," and "agent of change" (p. 1032). Similarly, Cochran-Smith and Paris (1995) raise questions about how mentoring can move from knowledge transmission to knowledge transformation, in efforts to interrupt problematic conditions in teaching and schooling. These categorizations distinguish different purposes for induction, roles for mentors, and ultimately the kinds of knowledge mentors need.

The case of Maya and Rob describes a more activist mentor role. It also highlights the dilemmas of such a stance. Maya noted how stressful it was to have to continually navigate and advocate, sometimes putting her at odds with the school. She recognized that to do "subversive" work, she needed to maintain strong relationships with key educators. Finally, she worried that the focus on politics may have taken away from much-needed coaching on teaching. The politics brought her into conflict with her own mentoring role.

Moral and Identity Dimensions

Mentoring occasions highlighted in the case raise another dimension of political literacy not identified by the questionnaire: a moral component. The conflicts that initiate political activities are embedded in issues of morality—what is right and wrong in education. As new teachers develop beliefs about students and teaching, they come to see conflicts that arise between their own ideals and those in their organizational surroundings. Schempp, Sparkes, and Templin (1993) found that micropolitical issues confronted by beginning teachers pressured "new teachers to forsake their ideals and education and accept the conditions and standards of the schools as they presently existed" (p. 469). It was Rob's commitments to teaching literacy through a student-centered, balanced literature approach to meet the needs of his diverse students that caused him to reject the school and district's approaches. Similarly, it was his beliefs about the inequity of tracking that resulted in a conflict at his grade level. In her work with Rob, Maya continually highlighted the values at stake, providing language about the new teachers' commitments about "what is right," applauding him for his conviction to stand by his philosophy, and advocating for these principles with other educators. Thus Maya could disrupt the kind of novice accommodation that often results when new teachers become institutionally compliant and eschew commitments (Lacey, 1977).

The case spotlights that when novices find discrepancies between their values and the dominant ones in a school, it can support a "politics of identity," establishing or restoring one's identity as a teacher (Kelchtermans & Ballet, 2002). Thus another aspect of a mentor's political literacy is how it supports new teachers to develop a politics of their own identities, articulating their values, morals, and commitments.

APPLICATIONS AND CONCLUSIONS

Clearly Maya is a mentor who has thought deeply about political and organizational concerns. How might a program help mentors develop such complex understandings and ways of negotiating this complex terrain? LNTI participants, identifying their own discomfort with their level of organizational knowledge, made efforts to develop their repertoire of practice related to political literacy. In one activity, they assessed their own assumptions about political knowledge with reflective writing about what being political in the context of their induction programs meant and what their feelings were when others were "being political." They identified negative and positive meanings of these words in their work. They also "mapped" their organizational terrains, identifying a desired program-level outcome, forces and people for and against it, and their own sphere of influence for achieving this outcome. They articulated advocacy steps and role-played interactions.

Supporting new teachers is an enormous task. Yet without knowledge of how to read, navigate, and transform the organizational contexts in which novices work, a mentor's knowledge base is incomplete. Mentors cannot solely focus on classroom-based learning. They must also focus their lenses on the organizational contexts in which classrooms are embedded. Mentors' political literacy offers novices a way to act in the political climate of schools, to address inevitable conflicts with colleagues and administrators, and ultimately to move to define a professional identity. Rather than viewing politics as negative, this chapter explored how knowledge of the politics of school life can enhance mentors' repertoires of practice and foster development of novices.

NOTES

Acknowledgments. Thank you to the educators in this study, Anna Speiglman for her contributions to data collection and analysis, and Geert Kelchtermans for conversations on political literacy.

1. All names are pseudonyms to maintain confidentiality of respondents.

2. The questionnaire was analyzed by two researchers who developed codes that emerged from the data (Miles & Huberman, 1994). The researchers then separately coded and compared results, reaching 90% interrater reliability. Data from the 1-year case study included: 13 transcribed audiotaped interviews with the novice and his mentor, principal, and colleagues (1–1.5 hours each), and 6 transcribed audiotaped mentoring conferences (ranging from 40 minutes to 90 minutes each). Case study data were examined and coded based on questionnaire codes. I developed vignettes that highlighted dimensions found in the questionnaire, as well as new categories, such as challenges and moral issues.

3. I use the terms *micropolitical literacy* and *political literacy* interchangeably. Micropolitics, as highlighted in the research, refers to the political negotiations within the day-to-day life of schools—the intraorganizational processes (Achinstein, 2002; Ball, 1987; Blase, 1991). Since some of the micropolitics of mentors' and new

teachers' experiences interact with macropolitical contexts (such as educational
policies at the district, state, or even federal level), I use the more inclusive term
political literacy for this chapter.

REFERENCES

Achinstein, B. (2002). Conflict amid community: The micropolitics of teacher collaboration. *Teachers College Record, 104*(3), 421–455.

Ball, S. J. (1987). *The micro-politics of the school: Towards a theory of school organization.* New York: Routledge.

Blase, J. (1988). The everyday political perspectives of teachers: Vulnerability and
conservatism. *International Journal of Qualitative Studies in Education, 1*(2),
125–142.

Blase, J. (1991). *The politics of life in schools: Power, conflict and cooperation.*
London: Sage.

Cochran-Smith, M., & Paris, P. (1995). Mentor and mentoring: Did Homer have it
right? In J. Smith (Ed.), *Critical discourses on teacher development* (pp. 181–
202). London: Cassell.

Feiman-Nemser, S. (2001). From preparation to practice: Designing a continuum
to strengthen and sustain teaching. *Teachers College Record, 103*(6), 1013–
1055.

Goodman, J. (1988). The political tactics and teaching strategies of reflective, active preservice teachers. *The Elementary School Journal, 89*(10), 23–41.

High Point: The Basics. (2005). Carmel, CA: Hampton-Brown.

Kelchtermans, G., & Ballet, K. (2002). The micropolitics of teacher induction: A
narrative-biographical study on teacher socialisation. *Teaching and Teacher
Education, 18*(1), 105–120.

Kelchtermans, G., & Ballet, K. (2003). Micropolitical literacy: Reconstructing a
neglected dimension in teacher development. *International Journal of Educational Research, 37,* 755–767.

Lacey, C. (1977). *The socialization of teachers.* London: Methuen.

Miles, M. B., & Huberman, A. M. (1994). *Qualitative data analysis: An expanded
sourcebook* (2nd ed.). Thousand Oaks, CA: Sage.

Open Court Reading. (2005). New York: SRA/McGraw-Hill.

Schempp, P. G., Sparkes, A., & Templin, T. (1993). The micropolitics of teacher
induction. *American Educational Research Journal, 30*(3), 447–472.

Tomlinson, C. A. (1998). *The differentiated classroom: Responding to the needs of
all learners.* Alexandria, VA: Association for Supervision and Curriculum
Development.

Veenman, S. (1984). Perceived problems of beginning teachers. *Review of Educational Research, 54*(2), 143–178.

Wang, J., & Odell, S. J. (2002). Mentored learning to teach according to standards-
based reform: A critical review. *Review of Educational Research, 72*(3), 481–
546.

CHAPTER 10

Mentors as Induction Leaders: Solving Organizational Challenges to Develop Effective Mentor Programs

Steven Z. Athanases, Lyn Nichols, Lisa Metzinger, and Ruth Beauchamp

Just as teachers face new challenges in moving beyond their classrooms to mentoring new teachers, experienced mentors face challenges as they assume positions of mentor leadership. These include developing mentor curriculum for new mentors, explored in Part II of this book. Also, however, challenges arise at the organizational level as these educators shape programs, guide mentors, and organize personnel who include new teachers, mentors, school administrators, induction leaders, district coordinators, and county office leaders. Challenges include creating a flow of communication and advocating for mentors and new teachers within often-complex systems, frequently with internal conflicts and competing needs and agendas.

We report from two case studies concerning organizational challenges impeding induction program development. The cases reflect lessons learned by program leaders from work with the Leadership Network for Teacher Induction (LNTI, see Introduction), involving ongoing professional development in program leadership and action research cycles. The cases used a range of data sources, including interviews with mentors, new teachers, and administrators; focus groups of mentors; surveys of mentors and new teachers; and records from mentor professional development sessions. Steven participated in workshops and summer institutes with LNTI, guiding data analysis and writing of cases. The other co-authors are program leaders who developed cases from collaborative action research on their induction programs. Together we analyzed what was important about these cases. We distill the cases into brief summaries, then glean principles and ideas relevant to wider audiences of mentors who may face similar organizational challenges in developing and maintaining induction programs that effectively serve mentors, new teachers, and their students.

The first case describes the challenge of shaping a nonhierarchical leadership style that can engage mentors in meaningful work and might foster shared leadership. The second case examines organizational challenges in a complex multidistrict consortium of mentors. In both cases, induction leaders confront organizational challenges and inquire into ways to reshape organizations to better support mentor development.

CASE 1: FROM HIERARCHY TO MENTOR BUY-IN: RESHAPING THE CULTURE OF A MENTOR PROGRAM

A painful fact one induction team had to face was this: one of their biggest obstacles was their own adopted leadership style, which conflicted with who they wanted to be as leaders. Lyn, Lisa, and colleagues were "in charge" teachers used to relying on themselves in their classrooms. As most school districts are structured as "top-down" systems, even with efforts to increase site-based management and to provide opportunities for teacher-led programs, leadership usually remains hierarchical. Just as teachers draw on what they knew as students—the apprenticeship of observation (Lortie, 1975)—so, too, do teacher leaders slip into the default mode of hierarchical leadership they have witnessed.

Though the team worked under district administrators who valued teacher input and fostered shared leadership and autonomy in programs they administered, the overall system at the time of this study was hierarchic.[1] District administrators had designated this team to be program "leaders"—who easily adopted leadership styles they had seen modeled by administrators they had worked under as teachers. Though team members considered themselves collaborative leaders in theory, a top-down model considerably affected their leadership practices. Operating out of alignment with deeply held values and beliefs causes stress, and the team felt the beginnings of burnout without realizing it. It became clear, when the group met in LNTI meetings and examined themselves and the literature, that a more community-oriented, less patriarchal model was needed for their work with teachers. They needed more authentic and democratic conversations. They also needed renewal, which differs from reform and restructuring in that it is a change within people, is internally motivated rather than externally imposed, and holds potential to sustain change efforts (Pellicer & Anderson, 1995).

The team developed a districtwide Teacher Leader Network (TLN) that they hoped might bring renewal, not just for the ongoing core group, but for the entire new teacher program and district as well. Beginning within their own sphere of influence and changing the culture of their teacher induction practice, they might provide a model that could lever change districtwide. This case, then, considers these research questions: (1) Can conscious efforts to increase teacher leadership capacity build a broader base of autonomous teacher leaders? (2) What effect can participation in a collaborative, community-based model of professional development have on development of teacher leaders?

Context of the Problem: Challenges of Leadership

Lyn and Lisa's Northern California school district had a relatively long history of new teacher support since 1988, when a district mentor participated in design and implementation of the California New Teacher Project and brought it to the district, instituting new teacher support as standard district practice. In 1993, the district became one of the first Beginning Teacher Support and Assessment (BTSA) projects with a grant to support 50 1st-year district teachers and new teachers' mentors. The program extended to support all 1st- and 2nd-year teachers, credential program interns from a partner university, and newly hired emergency permit holders—a total of 171 new teachers. Support and assessment grew increasingly complex and paper-intensive, and leaders felt overwhelmed by the workload, even with additional mentors. The hope was that through involvement in LNTI the team could increase teacher leadership capacity and teacher empowerment to build a broader base for leadership in teacher induction.

Data collected from new teachers indicated that the programs were successful, yet leaders critiqued their own work. One remarked, "Looking at the type of leader I wanted to be, one who fostered shared leadership, and the type of 'top-down' leader I was becoming, frightened me. The values I said I held and the way I behaved were not congruent." Another noted: "I was stunned to realize I was acting just like administrators I did not admire . . . who didn't share leadership with others. . . . It was becoming easier and easier to 'do the job myself' rather than rely on someone else." If this problem was not addressed, could effective mentoring be sustained? Since the program seemed overly reliant on this core group of leaders, what would happen if the leadership disappeared? Would the program fail? Evidence in the literature suggested that programs overly dependent on a single leader or core group of leaders holding the vision and bearing sole responsibility for success or failure were more likely to fail (Lambert, 1998).

Action Plan: Expanding the Leadership Base

To increase leadership capacity and empower teacher leaders, the team created a new role of mentor assessor. The plan was to identify areas of specific need (math and special education at the high school, for example) and a core of veteran mentor teachers within these areas who might want to expand their role from support only to support and assessment. Professional development in monthly seminars included ways to deepen peer coaching and communication skills, methods of observation and data collection, and skills in using formative assessment. Sessions were not top-down trainings, but seminars where participants could share what was working/not working. Participants provided feedback at each meeting to ensure that needs were being met and to sharpen direction for next sessions. The team hypothesized that creating the mentor assessor role would expand the leadership base and provide more buy-in from mentors to work with new teachers. They also believed that the method used for sessions would model collaboration for new teacher leaders. Also, creating a broader base of support and assessment would help the leadership team return to their original charge, envisioned 7 years earlier, of mentoring mentors.

Concluding that the mentor assessor role was increasing leadership capacity for new teacher support, the team looked beyond its own programs to others invested in supporting teachers to increase student achievement. Teachers on special assignment worked on English language development, literacy, technology, special education, and new teacher support, all somewhat independently at the same district office. It became clear that groups needed a process to work more closely to support teachers.

Funds were found and the program specialist for literacy became a member of the LNTI team, which then engaged all specialists and assistant superintendents for personnel and instruction. A steering committee formed, hammered out a vision statement, designed a process for recruitment into the TLN, and designed professional development goals. A constructivist professional development model emerged after potential participants were surveyed at a first orientation meeting to learn topics the group was interested in exploring. On average, there were 13 regular attendees at sessions, with varied leadership roles—department heads, consulting teachers, union leaders, digital high school program managers, and technology coaches. Each of five 3-hour sessions over the year began with establishing and revisiting norms for dialogue, and included time for professional reading, reflection, and discussion on key topics such as diversity and moral leadership. Sessions also included time for skill-building and learning leadership skills, including managing conflict among adults and dealing with difficult people. In addition to organizing a districtwide leadership focus, team members sought ways to foster collaboration and community where they could.

Inquiry: Did the Reculturing Work?

Did the model succeed in building a community of leaders as positive role models and change agents at their sites? Did leaders feel empowered and committed to creating conditions for collaboration, reflection, and ongoing learning? Survey, focus group, and observation data revealed participants' confidence levels in leadership skills, perceptions of program attention to preparing them in these areas, and the impact of the network on their work as teachers.

Program design. The team learned that teacher leaders needed a safe environment for discussion. Norm-setting needed to occur at the first session and be revisited at subsequent sessions to create and maintain members' feelings of safety. Second, leaders needed opportunities to reflect on reading and to discuss professional educational literature in small-group settings where everyone's voice could be heard. One middle school teacher noted, "Time flies because we've shared from the literature. When I hear the really wonderful things people are doing, it really motivates me." She later stated, and others agreed, "For me, the small group size has been helpful." An elementary school union leader said she attended because, "I value reflection. . . . This is a safe place to talk about major things that have a huge effect in the classroom."

Collaboration across grade levels. Collaboration and networking across grade levels and programs were highly valued by teacher leaders. One noted, "Talking with others with similar issues is so helpful." Another valued "cross-pollination" that occurred at training sessions. In a focus group, all 12 participants agreed that collaborating with teachers from other sites and grade levels was a reason they attended the leadership network. One valued, and others heartily agreed, that "there is time for collegial interaction between levels. I can hear what's happening at other levels and what's successful and think about how it applies to my level." A veteran union leader summarized: "We've carved out time for collegial interaction among all three levels. This is truly what collaboration should be . . . as professionals, not discussing the number of textbooks in a back room." The team concluded that collaborating and networking is crucial to the development of teacher leaders and that if given opportunity to cross-pollinate, they are more likely to take what they learn and apply it to their own situations.

Shared leadership is energizing. There was evidence of a behavioral shift among program leaders to a more collaborative, shared leadership. This shift motivated new leaders and provided a sense of renewal for the original team. A new mentor summarized changes she saw:

> Initially I felt that there was a lot of the first leaders sharing how things are, saying this is the culture, this is the way we've always done it. Then it was as if they had an epiphany about their leadership styles. Things changed instantly. I feel more powerful.

Team members committed to look for opportunities to share leadership in their programs. For the next retreat, input was sought from all involved teachers for program improvement. Over the year, teachers were provided with opportunities for input on program change and to take the lead in implementing projects. They also represented the program at state and regional meetings and presented work and/or findings at a retreat.

In a year-end survey, 66% of teachers involved reported that they strongly agreed with the statement, "I have had more input on program decisions since last year's retreat." One noted, "not having an agenda designed by someone else with 25 things that have to be covered is really nice. Instead of feeling bogged down and 'wasted' like I do after other kinds of meetings, I go out feeling charged and reinforced." It was evident that after the team had learned about best practices of teacher leaders, reflected on beliefs about leadership, and discussed their leadership styles, they were able to make behavioral changes that also benefited themselves. One noted:

> From the moment I realized that my actions did not match my beliefs, something shifted in me. Every day from then on, I watched for ways to give over responsibility and shift the leadership to others. For example, I found grant money to send interested teachers to conferences and pulled teachers in as guest speakers. . . . I applauded others at every opportunity and made it a rule to never do for others what they can and should do for themselves. I'm more jazzed to do the work now.

One mentor summarized:

> Since our program's shift to focusing on increasing leadership capac-
> ity of mentors, I am starting to find a new joy and passion. It is
> exciting for me to see teachers taking on more responsibility. Given
> the opportunity, they are adding to and enhancing our program in
> ways that our current leadership team either hadn't thought of or was
> too tired to come up with. They are asking to participate and contrib-
> ute, and they are doing excellent work!

Taking risks and seeking leadership opportunities. When shared leadership becomes the norm, teachers tend to take risks and seek leadership opportunities. One teacher said, "I found myself working with a staff member
who is considered 'high-maintenance.' Because of our having talked about ways
to communicate with difficult people, I was able to tell her what needed to be
said in a more professional and supportive way." Another member shared, "I
found myself working with the whole plant, including the administration and
custodial staff, to do team-building." Two program members from the same
elementary school told how they duplicated parts of sessions for instructional-
support-team meetings at their school. When others heard this, they sponta-
neously agreed that they wanted to do the same at their sites the next year.

Finally, a high school teacher told how she had taken a big risk toward
community-building. Her large high school was working on ways to increase
academic achievement of African American and Latino students, and teachers were beginning serious "courageous conversations" on equity issues. She
realized that opportunities to build trust and make the school safe for these
difficult conversations were badly needed. After some reflection, the teacher
chose not to go to the administration with her idea because she knew that if
it came from them, it would appear to be a top-down decision. Instead, she
took a deep breath and e-mailed the norms herself, along with ideas for their
use, to the over 240 staff members. One crusty veteran e-mailed back the
comment, "Where were you 20 years ago?! These norms for meetings might
have saved years of infighting in our department!"

That many teachers used new learning in their own settings affirmed
for the team that professional development in a safe, collaborative space that
included learning about and reflecting on leadership fostered an environment
that made teachers comfortable in using newly realized leadership skills. It
also was evident that enthusiasm engendered in the group might soon spread
to other parts of the district as well. However, not all participants experienced success in implementing what they learned at first try. A high school
teacher reported, "I don't think I've had much of an impact as a teacher leader
yet. . . . I still feel like a small cog."

Case Summary: Renewal, Reculturation, Interactive Professionalism

This case suggests that teachers may grow as leaders when they

• Perceive that a safe environment is established and norms maintain a culture of trust.
• Are provided with multiple opportunities to learn about the nature of leadership.
• Are provided with opportunities to reflect on their own leadership skills and attitudes.
• Have opportunities to expand their leadership.
• Have opportunities to collaborate with others.

The case also indicated that teacher leaders who participate in a group of this type may increase motivation and feelings of empowerment and develop a desire to use such a model in their own work as teacher leaders.

This new group of leaders reached out beyond its new teacher programs to leaders in other district programs to further support new teachers. They designed and implemented a program to support other leaders to reflect on their leadership and to deepen networking skills. These teachers reported taking their learning back to their sites and programs. In creating an environment for change, one adage states, "If you build it, they will come," but this case also seems to suggest the next step in this team's development: "If *they* build it, they will stay."

The team found that teachers who participate in shared leadership and collaborative decisionmaking experience renewal in and commitment to their work. There is an element of reculturing that can begin to occur where these teachers work, whether at a classroom, site, district, or program level. This renewal in teacher leaders can affect practice with new teachers who can be introduced to the idea of the "teacher as leader" in preservice education and that teacher leadership can be consciously modeled throughout a teacher's career. Many teachers, newly out of induction, are asked to assume leadership positions, heightening the need to create a culture of shared leadership and an atmosphere of teacher empowerment from the beginning of a teacher's career. Because of a shortage of administrators in California, teachers with only 4 or 5 years of experience have begun assuming administrative responsibilities. This underscores the need to focus on and model collaborative leadership at an early level, and to continue this focus beyond preservice and induction programs. As teacher credentialing practices change across the United States, the importance of creating a seamless program of professional development, starting at preservice and continuing beyond induction, is crucial. It is equally important that opportunities for reflection and collaborative leadership be threaded throughout all areas of formal and informal professional development.

CASE 2: ORGANIZATIONAL CHALLENGES IN A MULTIDISTRICT CONSORTIUM OF NEW TEACHER MENTORS

Sometimes large organizational structures provide multiple schools and districts with shared induction leaders and coordinated mentor curriculum and resources. A former teacher and mentor, Ruth assumed shared leadership of one such group, a multidistrict consortium organized at the county level, sponsored by the state-funded BTSA program. Moments before her first meeting with the consortium mentors she would support all year, with packets of classroom visit observation tools in hand, Ruth had butterflies in her stomach as if it were the first day of school. 4:00 came. 4:10. Her heart sank as the room was occupied with 8 mentors out of 79. How would the other 71 support their 129 new teachers?

Context: A Complex Countywide Consortium for Teacher Induction

When Ruth and her colleagues inherited this consortium, nine districts recently had dropped out. This left six very wounded districts with varied needs and mentors skeptical about what the consortium could provide them. Ruth realized that low attendance at required meetings was a symptom of larger problems she and her team set out to understand. The six remaining districts served 129 new teachers and 79 mentors within a 20-mile radius. There were 51 schools and site administrators, the smallest district with three schools, the largest with 23. Districts were urban and suburban, serving multiple socioeconomic, linguistic, and ethnic populations, and serving varied grade levels. Mentors were full-time teachers whose districts assigned them one to seven teachers to work with on a weekly basis.

Many educators were involved in this complex system. One of Ruth's assistants was responsible for program implementation and evaluation and training of mentors in state-developed formative assessment procedures. She also was responsible for budget, allocating resources, and collecting data on the program to maintain state funding, answering to the county office of education's professional development director, who answered to the assistant superintendent of instructional services. A full-time resource teacher assisted Ruth in program implementation, evaluation, and training while supporting mentors in monthly networking and support meetings and the new teachers in bimonthly networking and support meetings. An advisory committee consisted of mostly assistant superintendents from the six districts, who met with consortium leaders on a bimonthly basis and received frequent e-mail contact. These district administrators were the main communication link to site administrators, mentors, and new teachers. Plans were in place to include on the advisory committee teacher union members, as well as faculty from local universities where teachers could earn credit for participation in BTSA activities.

Action Plan and Inquiry to Strengthen the Consortium

Since districts had dropped out of the consortium and meetings were poorly attended, Ruth and her leadership team developed an infrastructure and better communication. They established a comprehensive list of key contacts per district; scheduled regular meetings; and wrote program literature (brochure, newsletters, and handbook). They developed a master calendar of scheduled training and meeting times and a workable budget. For communication, they began building relationships with the advisory committee and created a database and group e-mail address book to ease access to all. Most important, they launched an inquiry project, collecting data to survey needs regarding communication and buy-in. It included site administrator surveys, mentor interviews, and a focus group with subject matter professional developers at the county office. Data were tallied and analyzed, and themes identified.

Organizational Problems Underlying the Consortium's Work

Three main problems emerged from data analysis. Following are brief descriptions of these and ways the team responded.

Lack of communication flow. Communication flow is vital for a program to establish buy-in and to convey information about protocol, procedures, and opportunities. The team learned that communication flow in the consortium was weak. Administrators reported hearing from the mentor consortium about its programs to varied degrees, many reporting that they received little or no communication over a 4-month period from August to November. One possible explanation was that some site administrators with few or no new teachers at their sites understandably heard little. However, mentors also had varied information about need to communicate with site administrators.

The lack of communication flow also arose from poor attendance at consortium meetings. Each group had low attendance at county-offered training sessions and meetings, having dropped nearly 50% at each level. The larger the group, the fewer number attended, with only 10% of mentors now attending and only 3% of new teachers present. The data may reflect a lack of trickle-down communication at each level about meeting times and locations. It also may indicate that school site and district professional growth offerings took precedence over county BTSA programs. Groups may have been conflicted as to which meetings to attend, or may have felt allegiance to their district and chose not to come. Some also valued meetings and trainings offered for their own people and valued less those professional development offerings off-site. One other explanation is that for many sites in the consortium, a commute to the county office although only 15 miles away, was long, deterring attendance. Also, besides attendance records, the team had no tracking or accountability mechanism to follow up with absentees, creating further absenteeism. Information dispensed at advisory committee meetings was not effectively trickling down or disseminated to new teachers, where it could make the greatest impact with students. The team realized the need to make themselves more available from the ground up with new teachers and to make a greater presence in districts at meetings for site administrators and new teachers.

Weak program alignment. Problems emerged regarding lack of consistency across programs, in ways that could impact teaching and learning in new teachers' classrooms. Mentors shared different amounts of information with site administrators, from "I don't share anything" to "everything," leaving school leaders with unequal access to information about support services provided, development of the new teachers, and values of the mentoring program. Data also revealed inconsistencies in how often mentors communicated with their new teachers. Most reported meeting weekly, some were in weekly e-mail correspondence, and others met only monthly with new teachers. Again, mentors may have lacked information about roles and responsibilities due to a breakdown in communication flow and lack of attendance at meetings and trainings. The BTSA program also was not aligned from school to school and there was no evidence of accountability; new teachers received different kinds of support, meaning students were not receiving equitable opportunities across classrooms.

In response to these problems, the team realized a need for more dialogue with districts and schools that were providing their own support for their mentors and new teachers. The team needed to establish ways to blend and synergize meeting and training offerings and to open these professional development opportunities across all consortium districts. They also wrote a protocol for mentors specifically about what they needed to communicate with site administrators and how often they needed to make contact with their new teachers.

Conflicting allegiance. For a program to succeed, members must be clear with whom to align themselves and with whom to be accountable. In the consortium, many did not know if they were accountable to the district or the county in their work, voicing confusion and pull between the two. One mentor noted, "I don't know exactly what is going on. It is not clear. The county says one thing, the district says another. It is confusing." An administrator asked, "Do I respond to district or county BTSA information?" Adding to lack of communication about accountability, there appeared to be conflicts in site, district, and county professional development offerings, as well as varied preferences for meeting sites, from county office, to local district placements, to repeated offerings in different parts of the county. Clearly, mentors wanted convenient locations for meetings. Districts and sites had responded by offering their own support meetings locally, again resulting in confusion about who was accountable to whom.

To clear up confusion, the team began discussions to spell out responsibilities of site, district, and consortium. The team also planned to work with districts on mentor expectations and training required to earn mentor stipends. They planned a tracking system and logs for mentors and new teachers in order to document time spent together and progress on formative assessment. They also began to network with union members and planned ways to have BTSA liaisons at each school site.

Case Summary: Managing a Consortium of Induction Programs

With challenges of a consortium of complex structures and different needs among and across groups, a beginning consortium might want to do several things. First, they may want to identify key players, survey needs, and address these in program development; take stock of resources and professional development programs currently available and incorporate what is already working; and develop communication channels directly to and across groups. Also, they may want to establish and communicate an accountability system for responsibilities of all involved; exercise flexibility and common sense in offering multiple meeting/training times and locations; and provide opportunities for teacher leadership by creating communication channels that trickle up as well as down. Finally, they may want to hire a lead mentor in each district to act as liaison, trainer, and advisory committee member; and create a tracking mechanism for quality control and accountability. Rebuilding a program is very difficult. Ruth and colleagues progressed yet continued to tread water. Nonetheless, these suggestions, culled from their action inquiry, suggest strategies for those taking on the challenge of leading large consortiumlike induction programs.

CROSS-CASE REFLECTIONS

These two cases offer lessons in organizational challenges of developing and maintaining quality mentor programs. The first case highlighted the challenge of designing leadership models for work in developing mentors. We have few models of how to develop leadership in school districts in ways that include teacher voices and invite multiple perspectives into shaping mentor programs. We need these, and the case reminds us that new teacher leaders may need to be reflective about their leadership approaches to engage more teachers in stepping up into leadership and mentor roles. Conceptions of leadership as hierarchical or collaborative hold implications for the kind of organizational culture into which we induct novices as well. Do we want to induct novices into a traditional hierarchical power structure that ignores their voices, or one more inclusive that seeks out new teacher leadership as well? Moreover, induction leaders have enormous capacity to leverage change in the profession because of the scope of their influence. These leaders can shape professional cultures up, down, and across educational contexts, influencing new teachers' practices and school and district cultures. Such a leadership role needs support and capacity-building for such ambitious organizational goals to be achieved.

Our second case reported organizational challenges in coordinating mentoring services across several diverse school sites and districts, with multiple players in need of strong communication flow, program alignment, and clarification of roles and allegiances. It highlights pitfalls of competing parties and conflicting professional development strategies. It also marks the need to confront programs not working, to inquire about reasons for failings, and to begin rebuilding. Without this kind of care, new teacher induction can fail to meet its loftier goals, slipping into unclear programs and, worse, meaningless busywork in educators' already burdened work lives.

Inquiry conducted by these mentor leaders enabled them, within a collaborative network of induction leaders, to sort out issues, analyze emerging problems, and plan for change. They were involved in formative assessment of their programs, supported by equally committed induction leaders. These cases point to issues that may run across many sites and may, with accumulating practitioner knowledge, yield generalized understandings of organizational land mines that await those designing mentor programs. This work also points to areas where induction leaders may need to be highly assertive change agents articulating ways in which educational organizations need to enable effective teacher induction work to proceed. The cases provide instances of individual groups engaging in inquiry into this work, reminding the profession that an investment in the learning of all youth requires an investment in mentoring new teachers, which in turn requires an investment of time and resources to develop quality induction programs and leaders who can serve all parties and, ultimately, all K–12 youth.

NOTE

1. The district more recently chose a new superintendent and assistant superintendent for instruction who are working to foster more collaborative leadership.

REFERENCES

Lambert, L. (1998). *Building leadership capacity in schools.* Alexandria, VA: Association for Supervision and Curriculum Development.
Lortie, D. (1975). *School teacher: A sociological study.* Chicago: University of Chicago Press.
Pellicer, L. O., & Anderson, L. W. (1995). *A handbook for teacher leaders.* Thousand Oaks, CA: Corwin Press, Sage Publications.

CHAPTER 11

Designing Mentoring Programs to Transform School Cultures

Janet Gless

Into what educational cultures do we induct new teachers? For what purposes? Beyond creating mentoring programs and development to address beginning teachers' needs, we need to consider organizational contexts in which mentoring programs are embedded. If we want schools where collaboration, thoughtful examination of practice, and honest reflection on student learning are common, then we need to develop both mentors and new teachers who can challenge the status quo. Program leaders ready to embrace this transformative vision need to examine their program structure, integration with other reforms, program leadership, and the quality and role of mentor teachers.

　　Drawing on over 20 years of work with beginning teachers, mentors, and induction leaders, I focus here on the concept of transformational mentors who can help reculture schools while promoting the highest-quality classroom practice. Mentors must be able to operate at four levels:

1.　Situate mentoring in the beginning teacher's classroom practice and students' learning.
2.　Foster collaborative learning environments for new and veteran teachers in schools.
3.　Forge new relationships with educators.

Mentors in the Making: Developing New Leaders for New Teachers, edited by Betty Achinstein and Steven Z. Athanases. Copyright © 2006 by Teachers College, Columbia University. All rights reserved. Prior to photocopying items for classroom use, please contact the Copyright Clearance Center, Customer Service, 222 Rosewood Dr., Danvers, MA 01923, USA, tel. (978) 750-8400.

4. Conceive of their role as teacher leader, conscious of the role's potential power.

I consider challenges and opportunities at each level.

FOCUSING ON CLASSROOM PRACTICE AND STUDENT LEARNING

Transformational mentoring begins in classrooms. It requires that mentors develop knowledge of each novice's level of practice, unique professional context, and students' needs. In contrast, a typical program model uses a full-time teacher to mentor a novice at the same school. For example, Nicole, a 20-year veteran, is asked to mentor a new colleague, Phillip, receiving a stipend of $750 per year. Nicole has 2 release days each year to observe Phillip's classroom and can use another 2 days to invite Phillip to her own classroom or to visit another veteran teacher. Conversations focus on challenges Phillip faces, solutions Nicole offers based on experience, curriculum planning, and sharing resources. Meetings often start at 3:00, and since Phillip coaches sports 3 days a week, Nicole's time with Phillip is often just a few minutes' check-in on how things are going. When the two manage a longer meeting, the focus often remains on challenges Phillip encountered that day. Nicole has little first-hand knowledge of Phillip's teaching practice, and because casual visiting of colleagues' classrooms is not a part of their school's culture, she has only observed him by chance when she dropped by to exchange information.

Buddies down the hall, although welcome sources of social support, do not represent a transformational model of mentoring. Yet even in programs where veteran teachers are released to mentor, classroom-based mentoring can be challenging. First, even the most carefully selected veterans are products of the existing culture. Often the finest practitioners have had little experience observing another teacher teach. In our New Teacher Center's (NTC) local induction program, where we employ full-time released veteran teachers to mentor, we selected a 30-year veteran math teacher widely acknowledged as the finest in his district, if not the county. He confided that in 30 years he had never observed another teacher teach.

In schools where classroom practice is a private act, what space exists to articulate to others what one knows about best practice? Frank, a 17-year middle school veteran and newly selected mentor, confided his vulnerability in this new mentoring role since he didn't know how to talk about his teaching. It was easy talking to students, but to other adults? Programs must ask, how will mentors learn to articulate what they intuitively know? Some teacher development initiatives recognize the need to help teachers develop professional language. Examples include the Interstate New Teacher Assessment and Support Consortium (INTASC) and the National Board for Professional Teaching Standards. California's approach to induction, the Beginning Teacher Support and Assessment (BTSA) program, found that having a common language (defined in CDE/CCTC, 1996) helps mentors develop confidence about what they know and a way to communicate it effectively.

Another challenge of this new mentor role is the burden of having solutions to the beginning teacher's dilemmas of practice. This can weigh heavily on a new mentor's mind and can be counterproductive to establishing a collaborative partnership. Mentors confide their fear that they won't "know the answers" and often are relieved to hear that they are not responsible for fixing all their beginning teachers' problems but for supporting teachers in finding solutions. Publicly acknowledged as expert in a culture that values knowing answers, veteran teachers understandably find it strange to be in a new teacher's classroom where they have little direct control. More than one mentor–beginning teacher relationship has been jeopardized by the mentor's struggle with this dilemma. The mentor often becomes overly directive, undermining the beginning teacher's fledgling autonomy; the mentor's suggestions and solutions lead to mixed results due to the new teacher's developmental level or personal teaching style; or when the beginning teacher shows reluctance to adopt a proffered solution, the mentor concludes that the new teacher is resistant.

Helping mentors adopt the stance of co-learner and inquirer into practice is an essential aspect of transformative mentoring. Yet it is hard for mentors who have been selected for acknowledged expertise to become learners alongside novice colleagues. This involves a courageous shift in professional identity and a public vulnerability uncommon in current school cultures. Programs adopting a mentoring model based on formative assessment of a beginning teacher's classroom practice help mentors shift from a "fix-it" approach to that of ongoing learning guided by a deeper understanding of the new teacher's professional strengths and challenges.

FOSTERING COLLABORATIVE LEARNING ENVIRONMENTS FOR NEW AND VETERAN TEACHERS

Teaching can be isolating, with doors shut and professional dilemmas and successes kept private. Despite a goal of collaborative school cultures, veteran teachers often have not had an opportunity to develop skills of collaboration. In transformational mentoring contexts, mentors must be able to help a new teacher navigate the existing culture of concealment while they support a new way of being in schools. It requires a delicate balancing act for mentors *and* new teachers.

Unfortunately, in their desire to protect new teachers, mentors often discourage exactly those behaviors that hold potential to help create new learning communities in schools. Some explicitly have counseled new teachers not to speak up at faculty meetings or to make public their successes or challenges, lest they be perceived as "upstarts" or "know-it-alls." The pervasive fear of making one's practice public still characterizes schools, and new teachers quickly learn these prevailing attitudes.

Transformational mentors, however, understand the importance of helping novices develop a professional voice that can support the emergence of new cultural norms, without undermining novices' credibility with colleagues or jeopardizing their professional standing. Kelissa, a 2nd-year mentor, was at times overwhelmed by her new teachers' needs. She also noted that their concerns and challenges often were similar, so she brought five K–2 new teachers together at her home to look at student work. By exploring curriculum and grade-level expectations for student work, learning needs of students, and possible ways to address them, Kelissa and her group worked on skills of professional dialogue. The first meeting was so successful that she brought them together six times that year. Although she guided the first meeting, teaching her mentees a protocol for looking at student work, over time Kelissa did less facilitation. The teachers were learning to facilitate rich conversations about teaching and their students' learning.

However, we found in the Santa Cruz New Teacher Project (SCNTP) that as novices exited our 2-year induction program they were distressed by the loss of regular, structured opportunities to talk about practice with other teachers and struggled to find ways to re-create the collaborative partnership they had had with their mentors. The SCNTP capitalized on this dilemma and now advises mentors about how they can influence school communities where they mentor. The possibilities range from inviting veteran teachers at the same grade level to join in a protocol-framed discussion of lesson planning, to simply inquiring if a new teacher can visit a veteran colleague to observe effective instructional strategies of one kind or another. Sometimes mentors attend grade-level or subject-area meetings with a new teacher to find ways to foster collaborative discussions of practice that will continue long after the mentor's job is done.

Transformational mentoring does not frame its charge merely as survival of new teachers for the first 1 to 3 years but as changing school cultures so that all teachers feel supported across a career span. There are two important implications for mentors and induction programs: (1) beginning teachers must be inducted so they see opportunities for ongoing professional learning in their own classrooms and schools; and (2) mentors must intentionally support developing autonomy of new teachers by helping them forge links with colleagues that feature collaboration and teacher learning and will replace the mentor when the induction period is done. Beginning teachers need opportunities to develop their professional voices in sheltered and structured environments. However, transformational programs and their mentors use new teacher seminars to teach skills that foster collaborative cultures:

- A focus on student data and student learning.
- Use of nonjudgmental, low-risk feedback.
- Questioning strategies that foster inquiry and curiosity.
- Acknowledgment of multiple perspectives and alternative approaches.
- Ongoing commitment to student learning.

As a 1st-year mentor, Maritza brought a visible laminated copy of collaborative mentoring language to her meetings with new teachers. The SCNTP has found that clear mentoring protocols structure and promote focused, collaborative dialogue among mentors and new teachers, rather than mere show-and-tell talk. Malcolm, a high school language arts mentor, coached new teachers on how to speak up at faculty meetings in ways that would not alienate their already somewhat disenfranchised colleagues. He did not discourage them from sharing opinions and insights but taught them about the complexity of change and its slower pace. Occasionally, Malcolm accompanied a mentee to a meeting, and together they would debrief what transpired and how they could, together, begin to shift norms and behaviors of the faculty or department group.

FORGING NEW PROFESSIONAL RELATIONSHIPS AS MENTORS

As they assume a new role, mentors begin to forge new relationships with colleagues, university supervisors, and administrators. Creating these relationships is complicated, however, by prevailing professional cultures that discourage singling out any member of the educational community, perpetuating the notion that when teachers leave the classroom to work with other teachers or assume roles that differentiate them from the rest of the faculty, they abandon colleagues. Induction program leaders need to communicate clearly across the system what the mentor's role entails.

For example, the NTC currently is working with one of the largest school districts in the United States to launch a transformational, districtwide induction model staffed by full-time release mentors. The implementation team sought to define:

- How was the mentor going to interface with other staff developers or coaches who operated at school sites?
- How would the mentor communicate with site administrators?
- What would be the relationship between university supervisors for the many new teachers concurrently enrolled in credential programs?
- What other programs needed to be included?

Defining and communicating the mentor's role only happens if program leadership is clear about the purpose and vision of their induction model. If the program is truly focused on implementing a transformational model, then language used to define the mentor's role (and to select mentors) will differ from one in which mentors are used to acculturate new entrants into a system's schools. For example, Induction Program A (below) characterizes the traditional and prevailing mentoring model. Program B incorporates language of a transformational model.

The goal of Program A is to support and retain new teachers. A mentor's role is to help teachers feel welcome and successful and to introduce them to procedures, practices, and personnel in the school. Mentors share resources, information, and curriculum guidance; convene small groups of beginning teachers when needed; and provide much-needed emotional support.

The goal of Program B is to promote high-quality teaching while building strong collaborative educational communities focused on excellence and equity for all student populations. A mentor's role is that of "teacher of teachers," to support novices' entry into the profession while accelerating development of effective, autonomous classroom teachers. The mentor forms a partnership with new teachers featuring instruction and student learning. The mentor employs a variety of classroom-based mentoring strategies, including formative assessment to guide the teacher's development and the mentor's focused support. Mentors share resources, guide reflection, facilitate analysis of student work, collect observation data for teacher learning, and, as teacher leaders, advocate for policies and practices that support new teachers.

Differences in these program descriptions have implications for a mentor's relationship with site administrators. Program A seeks to ensure continuance of a school's current practices and will ease transition of novices into teaching. The relationship between mentor and site administrator likely will be traditional, with the mentor serving as conduit for information from administration to new teacher, or with the administrator relying on the mentor to support existing norms and practices. The mentor may or may not need to be an exemplary teacher to perform the functions and may or may not be considered a teacher leader. In fact, in many programs the role of mentor is haphazardly assigned or delegated. Large urban school districts and hard-to-staff schools often have difficulty finding mentors to assume the role, even when modest stipends are provided. Under stressful circumstances, it often is unappealing to be a cheerleader for the status quo. Also, due to the higher percentage of new teachers in such schools there are fewer veterans to take on this additional responsibility. Furthermore, from the description above, little status is accorded the role of mentor, and it is unlikely that the mentor will be included in programmatic decisionmaking or development of policies to support new teachers.

Program B, however, identifies different expectations and a different status for mentors that, in turn, will lead to a different relationship with administrators. This program's mentors clearly focus on a new teacher's classroom instruction and successful transition into the profession. Continuance of current practices and policies is not even suggested. Instead, the mentor's role is to instill a set of practices that may or may not be the norm at a given site. Thus, the mentor is change agent (implied) and teacher leader (explicit). Like the site administrator, the mentor is a leader who supports best classroom practices. The clear focus on high quality instruction also requires the mentor to be an exemplary teacher who likely is already recognized as a kind of instructional leader. To succeed, the mentor must build upon this teaching credibility and develop a strong relationship with the site administrator, characterized by collegial independence and interdependence. To succeed in creating "collaborative learning environments" or in advocating "for practices and policies that support new teachers," mentors will need the support of site (and district office) administrators. In addition, Program B describes how mentors' work requires a specific knowledge base unique to the role and that will distinguish them from other teachers.

The challenge confronting induction programs that seek to build a strong transformation model is that teachers do not always possess leadership skills to communicate effectively with administrators other than in the manager–worker model. At the NTC, we broaden our mentor curriculum to include instruction, protocols, and tools for communicating with administrators. The mentor is encouraged to talk regularly with administrators while maintaining confidentiality of the mentor–beginning teacher's work. Mentors also are taught to articulate their role as an advocate not only for new teachers but also for a new vision of collaborative school communities and best practice across the site, a vision that is in most cases shared by the site administrator.

This collaborative focus requires that mentors learn to use new language with administrators *and* when talking about administrators. Districts where veteran teachers know the language of "us-and-them" need to hear new language and be reminded that mentors have to walk and talk in ways that will help create the new order they (and their program) envision. This is especially challenging in districts where paternalistic administrative models dominate; where there is a strong history of confrontation between district and teacher organizations; or where teachers accord administrators an unnecessary, all-powerful status, thereby ceding their voice and power. When mentors are approached by principals in ways that might compromise their relationship with a beginning teacher, they need to be able to clarify that concern, with respect for the needs of the site administrator. When a full-time release mentor is asked to assume additional duties beyond those of supporting new teachers, the mentor needs ways to point out the importance of support for new teachers and how it further supports the site's need for quality instruction and successful new teachers. These new relationships require that mentors have a clear understanding of who they are and how they fit into the system.

UNDERSTANDING THE POWER OF THE MENTOR ROLE

Developing mentors as educational leaders and change agents begins with recruitment, especially important in districts or programs where prior practice has involved a buddy–mentor model. Every communication about the program and the selection process must convey to the veteran teacher that the induction program is intended to impact classroom practice and involve new relationships. Outstanding veteran teachers are hungry for new leadership roles and opportunities to improve teaching and learning in schools. Unfortunately, systems offer few such roles to the veteran teacher other than school administrator or a limited number of "teacher on special assignment" opportunities, roles many veterans feel take them away from things that have kept them in the profession—interacting with students and classroom instruction.

In programs that adopt a full-time release mentoring model, mentors have potential for far greater influence than ever before in their professional lives. Most struggle with their departure from the classroom and the realization that they are no longer working with students but begin to understand that they now might impact lives of many more students as they work with 12 or 15 new teachers in classrooms.

This work also means understanding how policies and institutional practices influence a novice's success. It means developing a systemic perspective far broader than that of most classroom teachers. This means being aware of new teacher resources, colleagues who can model classroom strategies and curriculum knowledge. This perspective involves knowing that successful mentoring depends upon site administrators, induction program leaders, novices' colleagues, and fellow mentors. As advocate and resource for new teachers, the mentor must be aware of what to advocate for and the resources available to offer.

IMPLICATIONS FOR PROGRAMS

For induction programs to be transformational in ways outlined, they will need to create or have in place several things.

A Clearly Articulated Vision of Program and Mentor's Purpose

Without a clear understanding of what program leaders want to accomplish, an induction program, like any other endeavor, will be reduced to a "quick fix" or weak intervention with little impact. Yet too often, unambitious state policies encourage mentor programs to become nothing more than "mentoring lite" (Moir, personal communication, 1998). Broad state mandates for universal mentoring for novices without accompanying funding set sights far too low and encourage a culture of compliance. Recently, a program director in one state announced with pride that her district was "100% compliant" and that every beginning teacher had a mentor. Further conversation revealed, however, that no mentors had received training, a mentor job description did not exist, and many mentors were appointed by site administrators pressured to submit particular mentor names to the district office.

Induction programs that seek to transform classroom practice and school cultures need to say up front that that is their goal. Program designers need to bring together groups to help develop, buy into, and support this vision. Without cooperation of the broader educational community, the induction program can become isolated and marginalized within the system. Once the program's vision is clearly articulated, it becomes the responsibility of program leaders to keep that vision front and center, asking themselves:

- Are our vision and goals still the most powerful and appropriate for our program and schools?
- Do our mentors, beginning teachers, teacher associations, administrators, and greater community know what these goals are, and do they share in our vision?
- To what extent is our program advancing our achievement of these goals?
- Are we making the right choices? Are we strategic?
- What do we need to change to be more successful?

- How is our program modeling the norms and practices we want to establish in schools through our induction model?

This vision and clarity of purpose need to guide every programmatic decision, beginning with mentor selection.

Recruitment and Rigorous Selection of Mentors

The critical first step for an induction program is recruitment and selection of mentors. Many programs fail to achieve potential due to lack of high-quality candidates for mentoring. Exemplary veteran teachers do not always step forward into the role. Cynicism, prior mentoring policies or practices, mistrust of the system, or fear of leaving the classroom are often impediments. Many of these attitudes can be mitigated when recruitment and selection are open, well communicated, clearly delineated, and characterized by high standards.

One large urban district, in partnership with the NTC, implemented an induction model seeking to be transformational. Once the selection process was developed collaboratively by district and union, an intensive recruitment process was initiated and involved every imaginable network, including administrator association, teachers' union, partnering colleges and universities, site and regional administrators, and informal educator networks. Program leaders held informational sessions across the district to explain the program and its vision. Job announcements were e-mailed repeatedly. Over 1,700 candidates applied for approximately 350 mentor positions within a mere 60 days.

Getting the right people on board also depends on a selection process that ensures that key players agree on the kind of mentor being selected. This may require risky shifts from prior practices that selected mentors based on who was available or affiliated with the power base, had most seniority, or had served as a mentor (informal or formal) in the past. Clear selection criteria help. A rubric can articulate the knowledge, skills, and dispositions mentors need to become transformational mentors required by the program; it also helps to convey and reinforce the program's vision.

Finding ways to elicit prospective mentors' knowledge and expertise is also important. When time and resources permit, classroom visits to assess best practice help if selection committee members understand clearly exemplary levels of classroom practice. In one case, a staff development and mentor program coordinator realized there were discrepant assessments of a teacher's practice by selection committee members. To foster greater consistency, she instituted a daylong course in identifying and assessing best instructional practice.

When classroom observations are not possible, induction program leaders need a system for validating candidates' expertise. Careful interview procedures and references suffice if review panel members are clear about the type of mentor sought. The SCNTP has included a brief role-play between mentor candidate and a novice teacher, allowing interviewers to learn how the mentor might engage colleagues in thinking about practice. This demonstrates dramatically whether the candidate is predisposed toward inquiry and learning or to advice-giving where the new teacher is a deficient practitioner who needs remediation.

Ongoing Support to Perform the Role of Mentor

Programs interested in transformational induction must recognize that most veteran teachers, however talented in the classroom and however skilled with interpersonal relationships, will need ongoing professional development to accomplish ambitious goals. Educational leaders have an opportunity and an obligation to make schools and classrooms very different learning communities from those that came before. We have two choices: wait for others to do it for us, or imagine and construct programs that can help create schools we want and teachers our students deserve. New teacher induction can be a powerful reform initiative and each new teacher an opportunity to transform the system—if we seize these golden opportunities.

REFERENCE

California Department of Education/California Commission on Teacher Credentialing. (1996). *California standards for the teaching profession.* Sacramento: California Department of Education.

Toward Effective Mentoring: Future Directions for Theory and Practice

Betty Achinstein and Steven Z. Athanases

As educators we continue to invoke Homer's image of the mentor who educates, supports, and guides the novice. However, development of the role in the context of teacher induction has needed careful reconceptualizing based on more complex understandings of the nature of new teachers' work and professional circumstances, a theoretical body of research on the knowledge base of teaching, ambitious conceptions about and goals for induction and the profession, and images of the possible from the field of mentoring. This book provides a start on such work. The chapters have explored three cross-cutting themes:

1. Mentors as ongoing learners and inquirers into their practice.
2. The need to reconceptualize mentors' knowledge base.
3. The need to understand mentors' roles as educational leaders and agents of change.

In our concluding remarks, we draw on those themes as we identify future directions for practice, policy, and theory.

INVESTING IN MENTOR DEVELOPMENT

That mentors are not born but made and are continually in the making holds implications for both policy and practice. First, policymakers who advocate proliferation of induction programs without adequate support and resources for ongoing professional development of both mentors and novices undermine their policy goals of improving the quality of new teachers' practice. Skeptics may challenge the cost of comprehensive induction support and extensive mentor professional development. Yet they also need to consider the costs of the revolving door and the benefits of improved retention, teacher quality, and student achievement. As discussed in the Introduction, recent research on one comprehensive induction and mentoring program that provided high-quality weekly mentor professional development resulted in long-term retention of its novices and teacher quality effects on student outcomes. Strong and St. John (2001) reported finding 89% of novices in that program remained teaching in the classroom and 94% remained in education after six years, and Fletcher, Strong, and Villar (2004) demonstrated that classes of new teachers supported by that mentoring program demonstrated achievement gains similar to those students in classes taught by more experienced teachers.

For practice, the kinds of professional development offered to mentors matters. That means providing meaningful contexts for learning beyond quick-fix training workshops focused on limited conceptions of the novice learner. Inquiry takes time and necessitates cycles of work. Moreover, the content of such professional development must reflect the complexity of the knowledge base needed for mentoring. Rather than a reductive approach to teacher development focused on emotional support and advice-giving, the kinds of reform-focused teaching expected of novices must be supported by informed conceptions of mentor development. Curriculum for such work must foster bilevel understandings (focused on teachers and students) of learners and learning; curriculum and teaching; and contexts and purposes. This book highlights several key domains of mentors' knowledge that need extensive development: formative assessment, pedagogical learner knowledge, antiracist mentoring, mentoring stances, adapting curriculum to local needs, subject matter expertise, curriculum of mentoring, political literacy, and leadership development.

When mentors step up to leadership roles, they need new structures to support inquiry at the programmatic level. Programs need to tap and develop new leaders experienced in inquiry, and then they need to have support for their own inquiry. Many chapters in this book are drawn from a network that engaged in ongoing support for these induction leaders to design action inquiry projects that could deepen and reform their work. Ultimately, inquiry has to go on at three levels. There has to be programmatic and resource support for inquiry at the teacher level, mentor level, and teacher induction leader level. This theme highlights the need for professional learning communities, providing opportunities for collaboration, exploring practice among peers, multiple perspectives, critique, and ongoing inquiry.

BUILDING A PROFESSIONAL KNOWLEDGE BASE OF MENTORING

This volume contributes to theory-building and informs directions for future research. Reconceptualizing the knowledge base of mentoring challenges underdeveloped perspectives of the work of mentoring. This volume provides a more robust portrait and examination of the complex and multidimensional knowledge base. For example, the organizational context domain has often remained unexamined or evaded in the literature. Too often the act of teaching is cast as one behind the closed door, stripped of consideration of its multiple embedded contexts (McLaughlin & Talbert, 2001). Shulman's work (1987) helped us understand ways in which context shapes a teacher's work with children, and Ladson-Billings (2001) and others have helped us understand the multiple layers of culture and communities as these also impact a teacher's work. However, left unexamined has been a conception of what the embedded contexts look like for the mentor guiding the novice teacher.

Future research and theory-building is needed in the realm of mentor knowledge. The chapters in this book highlight the power of looking to practitioner knowledge, wisdom of practice as a rich source for such inquiry and theory. We need to collect understandings from promising programs from the United States and beyond. These insights from within the profession can provide a theoretical frame to help us understand the nature of expertise needed to engage in this vital work of mentoring new teachers for a new profession.

GROWING EDUCATIONAL LEADERSHIP TO TRANSFORM THE PROFESSION

Also important for practice is that mentors need support and development to reenvision their roles from local guides to critical agents of change (Feiman-Nemser & Parker, 1993). This involves developing their own critique of educational institutions and building a repertoire of critical practices—for example, in supporting equitable outcomes. Furthermore, educators who take on leadership roles need to think about larger purposes of their induction program and the often hidden perspectives that underlie dominant approaches to induction, namely retention and socialization into the status quo. Mentors and induction leaders need support in managing and negotiating the tensions of upholding a critical perspective while sustaining ties with schools, districts, and local communities. Finally, schools and districts need to think about the organizational cultures into which novices are inducted, and the messages about professionalism that are sent when novices are given the most challenging working conditions. It is not enough to foster critically reflective mentors and novices if they are to enter toxic cultures that do not sustain their visions.

FINAL REFLECTION

We often think about our own new teacher experiences in the Chicago area as we examine the lives of mentors and their novices. As we look back at our own tallies of new teacher challenges that opened this book, we wonder how we would have experienced them differently with effective mentoring. How would careful mentoring have guided us to address the diverse needs of our diverse learners? We wonder what kind of knowledge about learners and learning, curriculum and teaching, and contexts and purposes we might have developed with more rigorous scaffolding, support, and critique. We do not romanticize that a mentor would have eased all of our challenges. Yet we also think about the kinds of learning opportunities that we and our students, as well as our schools, might have had access to, given a powerful mentor. We know a mentor would have challenged how we thought about teaching, interacted with students, and engaged in our profession. We also know that such a mentor could only have engaged us in this way given extensive professional development in a complex knowledge base of mentoring and a vision of transformative educational leadership. The authors in this book offer such visions of the possible, along with the struggles endemic to translating such conceptions into practice.

REFERENCES

Feiman-Nemser, S., & Parker, M. (1993). Mentoring in context: A comparison of two U.S. programs for beginning teachers. *International Journal of Educational Research, 19*(8), 699–718.

Fletcher, S., Strong, M., & Villar, A. (2004). *An investigation of the effects of teacher experience and teacher preparedness on the performance of Latino students in*

California. Santa Cruz: The New Teacher Center, University of California, Santa Cruz.

Ladson-Billings, G. (2001). *Crossing over to Canaan: The journey of new teachers in diverse classrooms*. San Francisco: Jossey-Bass.

McLaughlin, M., & Talbert, J. E. (2001). *Professional communities and the work of high school teaching*. Chicago: University of Chicago Press.

Shulman, L. S. (1987). Knowledge and teaching: Foundations of the new reform. *Harvard Educational Review, 57*(1), 1–22.

Strong, M., & St. John, L. (2001). *A study of teacher retention: The effects of mentoring for beginning teachers*. Santa Cruz: The New Teacher Center, University of California, Santa Cruz.

About the Editors and the Contributors

Betty Achinstein is a researcher at the New Teacher Center at the University of California, Santa Cruz. Betty conducts research on new teacher socialization, mentoring and induction, professional communities, and diversity and equity. She co-facilitated the Leadership Network for Teacher Induction, a reform network of induction leaders in Northern California. She also teaches on issues of diversity and education at UC Santa Cruz. Betty was Director of Member Schools at the Bay Area School Reform Collaborative. She received her Ph.D. from Stanford University Graduate School of Education, her master's degree from Harvard University Graduate School of Education, and her B.A. from Harvard-Radcliffe University. She taught middle and high school in Chicago, Boston, and New Jersey. Her book *Community, Diversity, and Conflict Among Schoolteachers: The Ties That Blind* (2002) addresses issues of professional learning communities. Some of her recent research articles address new teacher tracking, mentors' role in reframing novices' views of diverse learners, mentoring for equity, and mentoring relationships and new teacher learning.

Steven Z. Athanases is associate professor in the School of Education, University of California, Davis. His research and teaching focus on strengthening the teaching of English in urban public schools and on strengthening the preparation and mentoring of teachers for work with culturally and linguistically diverse students. Steven taught high school English in the Chicago area and has worked with practicing teachers in the areas of diversifying the literature curriculum, writing instruction, and classroom assessment reform. His articles have appeared in journals that include *Teachers College Record, Teaching and Teacher Education, Harvard Educational Review, Research in the Teaching of English, Journal of Literacy Research*, and *English Education*. Steven holds a Ph.D. from Stanford University in curriculum and teacher education, with a focus on language, literacy, and culture.

Jennifer Abrams is a professional developer with the Palo Alto Unified School District, California, and an independent educational consultant. Jennifer was a member of the Leadership Network for Teacher Induction. Jennifer taught high school English for nine years before she began work in professional development, where she coaches secondary school teachers and trains new teachers, supervisors, administrators, and other coaches. She also works nationally and internationally with public, private, and religious schools, organizations, and universities on supervision and evaluation, teacher leadership, and best instructional practices. The current focus of her consulting work is supporting educators in their work of having hard conversations. She received her master's degree in Education from Stanford University and a bachelor's degree in English from Tufts University.

Wendy Baron, Associate Director of the New Teacher Center, University of California, Santa Cruz, has led professional development efforts for beginning teachers and mentors in the Santa Cruz/Silicon Valley New Teacher Project for over 17 years. Wendy has a master's degree from Antioch College and an administrative credential from San Jose State University. She is co-author of two books, *Keys to the Classroom: A Teacher's Guide to the First Month of School*, and *Professional Development for Mentors, A Facilitator's Guide*. Wendy has also co-authored articles and research papers on the impact of mentoring on classroom practice and student achievement. Wendy led action research with lead mentors and principal coaches on the impact of working conditions on beginning teacher success through the Leadership Network for Teacher Induction. She works with districts and program leaders to integrate coaching, teacher collaboration, and professional development into the daily lives of teachers and administrators and continues to coach novice teachers and principals.

Ruth Beauchamp is Intern Coordinator and Beginning Teacher Support and Assessment (BTSA) advisor with the Peninsula New Teacher Project in San Mateo County, California. Her first experience in new teacher support was in 1993 when she participated in the first BTSA cohort in Sacramento as a 2nd-year teacher. After 8 years of teaching, Ruth became a BTSA advisor in Santa Clara County and took program coordination roles for BTSA and Intern Programs in 2000 and 2001, respectively. In 2002, Ruth moved to San Mateo to coordinate the Pre-Intern and Intern Programs. In 2003, Ruth earned her master's degree in Organization and Leadership and administrative credential from the University of San Francisco. Ruth was a member of the Leadership Network for Teacher Induction.

Barbara Davis has over 35 years of K–12 experience, as an elementary teacher, special projects coordinator, assistant principal, principal, and county office administrator. She is Assistant Director at the New Teacher Center, where she holds responsibility for outreach and dissemination of the Center's work. She co-facilitated the Leadership Network for Teacher Induction. She works with teachers, administrators, university faculty, and policymakers throughout the country as a consultant and presenter in new teacher professional development and in design and implementation of induction programs. Barbara has presented nationally on mentor professional development. She co-authored an article for the Association of California School Administrators' journal, *Educational Leadership*, on the principal's role in supporting new teachers and has developed and led workshops on the role of the site administrator in supporting mentors and acculturating new teachers into schools and the profession. She co-authored *Foundations in Mentoring*, a training manual for mentor professional development; authored *Using the Continuum of Teacher Development*, a guide for mentors in work with new teachers; and co-designed the New Teacher Center *Formative Assessment System*, a comprehensive program of tools and processes that help mentor and new teacher to move the teacher's practice forward.

Janet Gless has worked at the University of California, Santa Cruz since 1995, where she helped found the New Teacher Center (NTC). As an NTC Associate Director, Janet oversees the Professional Development and Dissemination Division's new teacher support efforts in 30 states. Her division assists state departments of education and district and school leaders to design and implement intensive teacher induction programs. She co-facilitated the Leadership Network for Teacher Induction. Janet has more than 25 years of experience as a classroom teacher, mentor to new teachers, induction program coordinator, and staff developer. From 1992 to 1995 she was a visiting educator for the California Department of Education, working with mentor teachers and consulting to induction programs throughout the state. Janet presents regularly at conferences on teacher development, induction, formative assessment, professional standards, and mentoring. She has co-authored book chapters, articles, and trainings on topics related to new teacher induction, mentoring, and teacher leadership.

Lori Helman is assistant professor at the University of Minnesota in the Department of Curriculum and Instruction. She specializes in literacy education and teacher leadership. A bilingual classroom teacher for 16 years, Lori was also coordinator of beginning teacher development at the New Teacher Center at the University of California, Santa Cruz and Literacy Coordinator of her school district. While at the New Teacher Center, Lori was a team member in the Leadership Network for Teacher Induction. Lori received her Ph.D. from the University of Nevada, Reno, where she studied the literacy development of young students in schools participating in a federally funded literacy support partnership. She has expertise in working with students from culturally and linguistically diverse backgrounds, and has been an author of a number of published articles relating to literacy assessment and instruction and teacher development, and how these apply to instruction for English language learners.

Gordon Jack coordinates the New Teacher Induction Program in the Mountain View–Los Altos High School District, California. Before he began work in professional development, Gordon served as a consulting teacher for 3 years for the Stanford Teacher Education Program. Gordon taught high school English for 8 years, in California, Spain, and Chile. In 2005, he returned to the classroom. He holds master's degrees in Educational Leadership from San Jose State University and Education from Stanford. Gordon was a member of the Leadership Network for Teacher Induction.

Virginia E. Johnson is a Program Director at the New Teacher Center at the University of California, Santa Cruz, and an adjunct professor at Holy Names University supervising interns and teaching intern seminars. She received her B.A. in Education from Fresno State College and her master's degree in Education from United States International University. She was a classroom teacher for over 20 years. After leaving the classroom she developed and provided staff development and served as a reading specialist, language arts leader, mentor, new teacher support liaison, and adjunct professor of reading. Her current focus is professional development in new teacher induction and in the New Teacher Center's Formative Assessment System. She participated in the Leadership Network for Teacher Induction on a team representing the Oakland Unified School District.

Susan Kwock is Dean of the School of Education and Liberal Arts at John F. Kennedy University. In more than 20 years as a teacher, curriculum specialist, and administrator in a large urban school district in the San Francisco Bay area, she has worked with diverse student populations and communities. The focal point of Susan's work is to promote social justice and educational equity to ensure that traditionally underserved students have access to high-quality learning opportunities and outcomes. Her role in the Leadership Network for Teacher Induction was one effort in this quest—to help identify effective culturally responsive attitudes and practices in mentoring beginning teachers who work in diverse urban classrooms, schools, and communities.

Enid Lee consults internationally on antiracist education. Through her consulting firm, she assists schools and districts in continuously restructuring for equitable outcomes for all students. She pioneered the professional development and school-change initiative *Putting Race on the Table*, designed to help teachers and administrators develop knowledge, skills, and will to create equity-centered classrooms. Her publications include *Letters to Marcia—A Teacher's Guide to Anti-racist Education* and *Beyond Heroes and Holidays: A Practical guide to K–12 Anti-Racist, Multicultural Education and Staff Development* (co-authored). As Visiting Scholar at The New Teacher Center, University of California, Santa Cruz, she worked on professional development with the Leadership Network for Teacher Induction. She is a Virtual Scholar with Teaching For Change in Washington, DC. Enid has an interdisciplinary master's degree in Caribbean Literature and Sociolinguistics from York University, Ontario, and was awarded an honorary Doctor of Laws by Queen's University, Ontario. Her current research features professional development for antiracist school leadership.

Judy McCurdy taught middle school for 13 years, then began supporting beginning teachers with a single-period release. This evolved into a full-time-release district mentor position to support beginning teachers and other coaches. During her 4 years as a full-time mentor, her district actively participated in the Leadership Network for Teacher Induction support activities. Judy's interest in administrative support for beginning teachers and their coaches was incentive for her to obtain her Tier I credential and master's degree in Educational Leadership from California State University, Hayward. She is vice principal in the Walnut Creek School District, where one of her responsibilities includes monitoring support provided for new teachers and their coaches.

Lisa Metzinger began work in education in 1987 as a 5th-grade teacher at Barnard-White Middle School in Union City, California. She also taught 7th-grade core, served as a site administrator, and coordinated the Beginning Teacher Support and Assessment (BTSA) program for the New Haven Unified School District, California. Lisa was a member of the Leadership Network for Teacher Induction. She is currently Coordinator for Personnel Services in New Haven Unified, as well as Director of the BTSA and Intern programs for the district. She received a bachelor's degree in Liberal Studies and a master's in Educational Leadership, both from California State University, Hayward.

Lyn Nichols received her B.A. in Education from the University of Northern Colorado and her master's in Educational Curriculum from California State University, Hayward. Lyn retired from the New Haven Unified School District, California, in 2003. In 30-plus years of service, Lyn was the creative force behind several innovations. While a teacher at James Logan High School, she developed the only Transpersonal Psychology elective in the nation and was instrumental in creating a 9th-grade required course on emotional health called "Lifeskills." Lyn worked with teachers as part of her regular teaching assignment, then as the district's first high school Beginning Teacher Specialist. Lynn was a member of the Leadership Network for Teacher Induction. She also worked with California State University, Hayward to design and implement a credential program called the New Haven Single Subject Partnership Program, which gained national recognition as the first credential pathway to integrate the School of Education's coursework with the California Standards for the Teaching Profession and to teach the objectives in a developmentally appropriate way. In 1991 Lyn was selected New Haven's teacher of the year. She works part-time as an educational and personal growth consultant and volunteers at Drew's Place, facilitating groups for bereaved children.

Suzi Riley has been an educator with the San Mateo Foster City School District, California, for many years. In addition to classroom teaching, she also has enjoyed work with new teachers. In 2000, Suzi became a full-time Beginning Teacher Support and Assessment coach. Since 2000 she also has been a Literacy Coach working with classroom teachers developing Writing Workshop across the district. Suzi is also a staff developer with the *Every Child a Reader and Writer* initiative. Suzi was a member of the Leadership Network for Teacher Induction.

Linda Shore is Director of the *Exploratorium Teacher Institute* and on the teaching faculty of the Exploratorium's *Center for Informal Learning and Schools.* Linda has expertise in science teacher induction, science teacher professional development, and inquiry-based science teaching and learning. She earned her bachelor's and master's degrees in physics from San Francisco State University and a doctorate in science education from Boston University. Linda received a Smithsonian Fellowship to work at the Harvard-Smithsonian Center for Astrophysics and to conduct research on the astronomy and physics conceptions held by K–12 science teachers and their students. She is the author of numerous articles on science teaching and learning, science teacher induction, museum-based teacher professional development, and popular science. Linda is co-author of the *Science Explorer, Science Explorer: Out and About* and *The Brain Explorer* books, designed to promote inquiry learning among children and parents.

Laura Stokes has worked with Inverness Research Associates since 1993, studying a variety of state-, federal-, and foundation-funded teacher leadership, professional development, and systemic reform projects. Projects include the National Writing Project; the Washington Initiative for National Board Certification of Teachers; Washington's Center for Strengthening the Teaching Profession; the American Museum of Natural History's Seminars on Science; the Teacher Institute's Beginning Teachers Program at the Exploratorium; and the Seattle Public Schools Expository Writing and Science Notebooks Project. Earlier, she directed the University of California, Davis National Writing Project site and the UC Davis Composition Program, co-directed the California Writing Project, and served as Assistant Director of the California Subject Matter Projects at the University of California Office of the President. She has a Ph.D. in educational policy from Stanford University, where her research focused on how teacher inquiry contributes to professional learning and school improvement.

Susan Totaro has been a tutor, teacher, and coach in the San Mateo-Foster City School District, California, for 20 years. She has been a Beginning Teacher Support and Assessment Advisor with the Peninsula New Teacher Project and with the New Teacher Center for 5 years. Susan was a member of the Leadership Network for Teacher Induction. She earned her teaching credential from San Francisco State University and in 1996 was named Teacher of the Year for her district.

Index

Humanistic perspective
  described, 7
  limitations of, 7–8
Humphrey, D. C., 4, 6, 38

Induction programs. *See also* Leadership
  Network for Teacher Induction
  (LNTI); Mentoring programs
  conceptions of, 5–6
  of Exploratorium Teacher Institute (TI),
    San Francisco, 98–101, 104, 106–
    107, 108n
  induction, defined, 5–6
  limitations of, 6–8
  need for, 3–4
  network of induction leaders and, 15–16
  new teacher participation in, 5
  in other countries, 5, 24
  subject-specific, 68, 96–108
  tensions in, 84–86
  transformational mentoring and, 165–
    175
Ingersoll, R. M., 3–5, 17 n. 1
Interstate New Teacher Assessment and
  Support Consortium (INTASC), 4,
  167
Israel, induction support in, 5

Jack, Gordon, 83–95
Japan, induction support in, 5
Johnson, S. M., 4
Johnson, Virginia, 83–95

Kagan, D. M., 7
Kain, J. F., 4
Kelchtermans, G., 14, 50, 124, 137–138,
  148
Kemple, J., 4
Kilbourn, B., 24
King, J., 50
Klein, S. P., 4, 11, 47
Knowledge base. *See* Professional
  knowledge base
Kuykendall, C., 90
Kwock, Susan, 83–95

Lacey, C., 148
Ladson-Billings, G., 11, 13, 39, 47, 179
Lambert, J., 154
Lankford, H., 38

Leadership Network for Teacher Induction
  (LNTI), 24–36, 83–95
  adapting mentor curricula and, 89–92
  assessment domains of mentor and, 25–
    34
  case examples of assessment and, 27–34
  challenges of leadership and, 153–154
  described, 15–16
  development of community of leaders
    and, 155–159
  equity as explicit and, 55–65
  expanding leadership base, 154–155
  inventing mentor curricula and, 92–94
  new teacher focus on learners and, 24–36
  organizational challenges to mentor
    development and, 151–164
  promises and challenges of assessment
    and, 35–36
  scripted mentor curricula and, 86–89
  shared leadership and, 156–157
  tensions in, 84–86
Learners, knowledge of, 17, 21–65
  bifocal perspective on, 47–50
  equity and diversity, 38–52
  formative assessment and, 23–36
  mentor and, 42–43
  professional development model for new
    teacher mentors, 55–65
  in targeting students, 12, 13, 48
  in targeting teachers, 12, 13–14, 48
Lee, Enid, 21–22, 55–65
Lieberman, A., 16
Little, J. W., 6, 7
Loeb, S., 38
Lortie, D., 39, 152
Low learners label, 44

Mackinnon, A., 11, 13, 21, 49
Making Equity Explicit (workshop series),
  58–63
  equity principle in, 61–63
  goals of, 59
  historical perspective in, 59–60
  institutional perspective in, 59–60
  processes in, 59–63
  responses to, 63–65
  social group membership in, 60–61
Materials, coping with lack of educational,
  128–129, 133–134
McCurdy, Judy, 83–95